LOVE LETTERS TO LISA

Bradley Scott Llano

NEWMAN SPRINGS PUBLISHING
320 Broad Street
Red Bank, NJ 07701

First originally published by Newman Springs Publishing 2023

ISBN 979-8-88763-960-4 (Paperback)
ISBN 979-8-88763-961-1 (Digital)

Printed in the United States of America

To Lisa, the one I call Beauty

Contents

Introduction

Let me tell you a story of love. Let me lead you into bliss and the wonder of a budding new couple entering into that most marvelous of institutions: marriage. Let me present to you the dreams of two hearts becoming one in a life that would test every fiber of their resolve. Let me show you the path of struggle, loss, and pain that led into the deep and darkened forest of madness. In spite of the waves of uncertainty that crashed in on this innocent young couple, plunging them to the bottom of the sea of despair, allow me to share with you their story of restoration. It is a love story.

This is a collection of love letters that are interwoven throughout the story of my darling Lisa and me—how we came to be, came together, came apart, and came back. I must let you know that all the letters you will read were actually written at the time of our reconciliation. I must also inform you that I did write love notes to Lisa from the earliest days, but sadly, those have not survived the years. If they had, you would certainly have seen them in this work.

This collection of letters has been therapy for Lisa and me as we have navigated the uncertain currents of the past, the rough waters of life without each other, and the uncharted seas of what comes next. At the end of this narrative will be the remaining letters that were not put into the story. They will be listed in the order they were written, with the hope that when you have read all the letters, you will have found something that you needed, whether it be encouragement, conformation, understanding, or agreement. You may be going through something similar, or you may just need to read a good love story.

My hope is that at the end of reading this work, you will have laughed, cried, sobbed, sighed, and realized that love—true intended love—can and will survive.

Chapter 1

WHAT IS A LOVE LETTER?

The Collins Dictionary has this to say about what a love letter is: "A love letter is a letter that you write to someone in order to tell them that you love them." Merriam-Webster boils it down to this: "A letter expressing a lover's affection." I submit to you that a love letter is the written expression of the heart's affection consisting of the outpouring of truthful emotional content from one to another.

Why do I ponder this? It is because of a love letter, to my dearest Lisa, written on the verge of reconciliation. That led to the ongoing pattern of love letters I continue to write, that I decided to present our story in its entirety. The love letter can present an avenue for communicating one's feelings and emotions in a way that is more intimate and passionate than the spoken word often allows. When I begin to write to the one I love, my heart proceeds to convey to my mind the things of love. My mind processes what my heart conveys, and words suddenly become joined together, forming sentences of proclamation, dedication, declaration, and devotion.

The love letter allows me to tarry and really think about what I want to say. There is something very therapeutic about taking the time and putting forth the effort to search out the words that will paint a picture for the reader and draw them in to the story your heart tells. I often get caught in the painting myself, feeling as if my lover and I are strolling hand in hand through the gently flowing meadow of my heart. The written word is strong medicine when administered properly. When that letter is written, delivered, and received, two hearts truly become one.

The love letters that I write to the one I call Beauty, who is my darling Lisa, are the backbone of this story. As I attempt to help you envision the sights, scenes, and settings of this story, I will interject the various love letters that I have written. These letters are the actual illustrations of my heart for the one I have loved and do still love most in this world.

A Love Letter to You

When you walked into the sanctuary, I was unable to breathe. I could barely speak the words I so longed to speak. You said "I do," and my heart leaped within my chest. When our bodies touched, I truly felt we were one. Our life together was interrupted and so prematurely put on hold. The pureness of our love was soiled by the corruption of this world. I died a thousand deaths at the thought of the chasm that lay between us. You never left my heart. I could not, would not, put you away. Now you speak my name and tell me that I have always been your true love. My heart once again leaps in my chest, and words vanish from my vocabulary. I am rendered mute, for I cannot find words eloquent enough to express my undying love for you. There are no words strong enough to convey my devotion to you. Let me then keep it simple. I love you, Lisa. I am in love with you. I have always been in love with you, and I know that I always will love you.

A letter about the beginning written so far after. Yes, a love letter. My love letters to Lisa will tell a story of true love, a story that spans so many years, a story that must be told. The spoken word simply will not do.

If you indulge me, I will attempt to briefly give you the why of the love letter. For me, the letters that I write now have their beginnings in the love notes that came to life during my courtship to Lisa.

It was 1987, and we were young, optimistic, and full of energy and enthusiasm. Our whole lives were ahead of us, and I was just beginning to realize that I wanted Lisa to be in my life forever. Little did I know what that would mean for the rest of my life. I found myself talking with her every time the opportunity presented itself, and I often created the opportunity if it did not present itself. When our schedules kept us from physically being together, I would write short notes to leave on her car windshield. Sometimes the notes consisted only of silly sketches, which I called my pictorial notes. Sometimes there were just a few words written on a small spiral notepad, such as "hope," "love you," "see you soon," or "waiting for you." Sometimes my marvelous expressions of affection were penned on a napkin—anything I could find to write on when the uncontrollable urge came upon me to let Lisa know that I alone was the one whose name was written in the stars next to hers.

Now, after many years, I still want to—no, *have to*—fill as much of her consciousness with my love, loyalty, devotion, and commitment as I can. I still talk to Lisa whenever I have the opportunity, and I still write those notes. However, the notes have become letters, and there is never enough time to tell her or write to her all the words my heart desires for her.

Chapter 2

BEGINNINGS

So how did we begin? Well, I was nine years old, and everything was new. My mother had recently gone through her second divorce, and as a single mother of two boys, she moved us from New Orleans, Louisiana, to a small country town in North Texas. Gainesville (with a population of more than ten thousand) was encompassed by a surrounding countryside complete with rustic farmhouses, barbed wire fences, and dirt roads that would wind through the fields and meadows where you could observe cattle and horses grazing or hay being harvested. In the city, you would find a courthouse, a movie theater, two main downtown streets, two grocery stores, one laundromat, two auto-parts stores, four elementary schools, one junior high, one high school, and a Montgomery Ward catalog store. Gainesville, Texas, was pretty much like any other small town in North Texas except for one thing: it was here that I met the love of my life.

I was a third grader in a new school in a new town, meeting new friends. One of these new friends was a kid named Bryan. Bryan and I became close friends, and we spent a lot of time at his grandparents' house. Nanny and Papaw happened to live in the same neighborhood that I lived in. One day, Bryan informed me that his two cousins would be coming over to play. I was eleven years old now, and these two cousins that were about to invade our buddy time were girls, and these girls were even younger than we were.

We decided on tag for the game and "stink bombs" for the name. The idea was when his cousins, Lisa and Amy, showed up and were forced upon us by the loving Nanny and Papaw, we would non-begrudgingly suggest the internationally recognized and most fun game in the world: tag. Obviously, the girls ("stink bombs") would be it. And to make it attractive to them, we allowed for the option where we would be stink bombs also if they managed to tag us. This was all well and good except that as time went on, I realized that I sort of wanted the older sister, Lisa, to catch me. I didn't even mind if I was made into a stink bomb in order to be caught and, more to the point, touched by Lisa. Bryan eventually caught on to my little ploy, and while he considered this a treasonous act, the flower of love was already beginning to grow between Lisa and me.

We continued to play from time to time at Nanny and Papaw's house, and as the years passed, we found ourselves in other social settings. We both attended the same youth group at our church, where we shared a very eclectic group of friends—friends that were starting to notice that Lisa and I were becoming more than just part of a youth group. Lisa and I were becoming part of something much larger than even she and I realized at first. I was beginning to desire more than Lisa's friendship, more than her companionship. I desired her laughter, her smile. I desired her inspiration. I desired her.

Please allow me to give a quick illustration. I mentioned our youth group and friends and a difference that was beginning to show. It was February of 1987, and our church was having its annual Valentine's banquet. The youth group was becoming a coming-of-age group and was starting to realize what falling in love meant. I had just turned twenty, and my precious little stink bomb was now sixteen, almost seventeen years old. Lisa was no longer a stink bomb; she never really was. Now, when I looked at Lisa from across the room, a new feeling began to rise up within me. I wasn't sure what this feeling was, but it compelled me to glance a little longer, smile a little larger, and maybe even leave a silly note: a love note.

I recall waiting after our youth service had ended one Wednesday evening so that I could ask Lisa if she wanted to be my date at the upcoming banquet. The longer I waited to have a moment alone with her, the more nervous I became. A lump began to swell up in my throat, and that's when my sweat glands kicked in. I was thinking, *Why was this so difficult?* I had talked to this girl for years, so what was the problem now? I said nothing that night.

The following Sunday after church, I caught her on her way to the parking lot and simply asked her if she wanted to sit by me at the banquet, and if so, I could pick her up and drive her there. Lisa shined as she agreed to my suggestion. That night, at the banquet, it was magical. It was not lost on a single soul that was there that evening that Lisa and Brad were on their first date. That very night, we shared our first kiss. Later that same year, I took Lisa to her junior prom, and it was official. We had begun.

Dating

Giddy, nervous, excited, anticipatory, hopeful—the emotions of new love. These were the emotions that were welling up inside me as I prepared for our first date. You were so beautiful and inviting, like the first day of spring. Your scent was so alluring, exhilarating…almost inebriating. You had most certainly captured my heart before I even realized it. You possessed a magnetism that drew me to you; it almost seemed primal. We were both so young and eager to really know each other. Though we were young, the time had come to embark on that wonderful time-honored tradition of finding your mate, the one you would spend the rest of your life with…dating.

My dearest Lisa, the one I call Beautiful, it seems an eternity since that first date and all the subsequent dates thereafter. You have remained as fresh in my memories and in my heart as that first electrifying moment in time when I knew I was going to ask you the biggest, most important question of my life: "Will you be my date?" This was the question that opened up a world of romance, passion, and completeness with my true soulmate.

Yes, there have been storms in our life. Yes, there have been obstacles on our path. We even believed, at one point, except for a dream world, our life together was over. It is so thrilling today to not start over but begin again as a new, fresh, rousing couple that can enjoy again the stirring of our hearts as we learn how to truly help, please, and love each other. We are becoming one. We are dating.

In 1988, there would be another Valentine's banquet, which would bring another milestone. But before I get to that, I must give the account of "the ski trip." The beginnings of Lisa and I were poetry being lived out day-to-day. The seed of love had taken root in our hearts; then it grew and it grew and it grew.

After Lisa's junior prom at the end of 1987, another event took place: the First Assembly of God youth ski trip. It was to be a great adventure into the snow-covered mountains of Ruidoso, New Mexico. I had never been snow-skiing before, and the thought of this first was so exciting to me. However, the excitement that I felt at going on this trip could not hold a candle to the excitement I felt at going on this trip with Lisa.

Within our youth group, I had developed another friendship that would also prove to be lifelong. A young man named Mike Mitchell was everything that you would expect a buddy to be, including being a little jealous of the increasing amount of time I was starting to spend with Lisa. I recall the day he expressed his concern that I wouldn't be able to tear myself away from Lisa long enough to have any quality buddy time.

During the planning phase for our upcoming journey into the snow-covered mountains of New Mexico, I would talk with Lisa, who thought I would spend all my time with my lunatic friend, Mike. Her belief, her fear, was that my time would be monopolized by Mike and consumed with absurdity and potty humor, leaving her in the lurch. Mike's concern, as I have already said, was that I would not possibly give up the lure of the fair Lisa for his inadequate company. I actually believe that the entire youth group was taking bets—in the most Christian way possible, I assure you—on who would pair up on the infamous ski trip of 1987. Something was happening. People were taking notice, and relationships were being put in order. A caste system was being formed, and love was obviously at the top.

I will tell you that I had every intention of going on this ski trip to have fun and play in the snow, learn how to ski, cultivate friendships, grow in the Lord, and not fall off a mountain. At this point, I have to inform you that I actually did fall off a mountain! But that is a story for another time. So friendships were cultivated, fun was had, and we all grew in the Lord a little on that trip. And I could hardly tear myself away from Lisa long enough to have any quality buddy time or any time that did not include Lisa's company.

Lisa and I were discovering just how much we needed each other. Once we arrived at the lodge and got settled into our rooms, the next order of business was to acquire the proper equipment for skiing. After this essential task was completed, it was on to ski lessons. One has to know the basics, and I was going to be there to catch Lisa every time she began to fall. Here's the truth. At every instructive moment, I fell, while Lisa was the picture of excellence, grace, and beauty. After graduating basic ski school, the whole class proceeded to ski our first bunny trail together. This was where my fair Lisa had the one and only fall I recall her having, which just happened to take out the entire class! As she sat up in the middle of the dogpile she had just so gracefully created, with snow in her hair and that look on her face that was a mix of embarrassment and shy enjoyment, I looked upon her and realized how much I was falling. Our youth group survived and returned home. The ski trip was over, but this was just the beginning.

Thinking of You

I think of you as I start my day. As I prepare myself for the day's work, my thoughts drift back to an image of your beautiful face, which has been forever imprinted on my mind. As I complete the mundane activities of the morning, I imagine us playfully calling to each other from room to room. This makes me smile, and it brings a warmth to my heart. Throughout the day, committing my thoughts to the tasks at hand becomes increasingly difficult because I wonder where you are and how you are feeling. I wonder if you are thinking of me. I wonder if you are happy or sad, working or playing, or maybe just waiting for me to send you a love note? When my workday finally comes to an end, I think of us sitting on a sofa together and holding each other as we relax and unwind. I think of calling you, and I do. Then we talk until the next day begins. We laugh, we cry, we talk sexy, and we finally say goodbye. When I think that I will stop thinking and go to sleep, you come to me in my dreams. I think I love you. I know that I love you, and I am thinking of you right now.

Now, about that next Valentine's banquet, this was perhaps the beginning of the biggest beginning that Lisa and I would ever have. It was now 1988, and this time, the banquet would be held at a restaurant in Dallas, Texas. There would be no church fellowship hall dinner, no Sunday-school class tables pushed together and covered with white paper tablecloths. This would be extravagant, elegant, and exquisite. This would be "the banquet." We were going all out to Mother Tucker's! Okay, so it was a burger joint, but it was a nice burger joint.

What was so special about this banquet? Nothing, except that this would be the venue for my proposal. Lisa and I already knew the path we were on. We already had plans for our future together. But beginnings are not beginnings unless they are marked by happenings, and what was to happen at Mother Tucker's on the evening of that Valentine's banquet in early 1988 was that I was going to ask Lisa to be my wife!

We had already talked about it, and I already knew that she would say yes, but there is something about having the perfect moment and witnesses and going down on one knee to hold up a diamond ring in one hand while taking the hand of your intended in your other hand to say "Will you marry me?" Every aspect of nature became clearer, sharper, more intense at that moment. I can still remember the celestial shades of tangerine that faded into a hot yet pastel pink, then powder blue to deep purple as if the night sky above bent down to kiss the early evening dusk. The sun was now beneath the horizon, its rays appearing just as though God Himself was shining all the spotlights of heaven upon us, signifying His approval of this most glorious moment. It was clear, and the first stars were starting to decorate the evening sky. We were in the third largest city in Texas, yet I heard no hustle, no bustle. The sounds of the city were somewhere else. I was hearing the ethereal choir of the leaves gently blowing across the pavement and the tunes of the first crickets as they performed a ballad for our love story. And I heard the most beautiful, most rapturous, most angelic voice I had ever heard say the single most powerful word in the universe: "YES!" This beginning has defined my life.

Sleeping on Me

When we embrace, it is one of the most comfortable feelings I've ever known. It is security, support, and sweet sensuality. However, when we are simply lying next to each other watching a movie, and I begin to hear that soft rhythmic breathing and I feel the warmth of your breath against my chest, I know that you have drifted off into that so-peaceful sleep that only lovers share. "When two are one and comfortable" doesn't begin to describe the feelings they feel for each other. This is the embrace that I remember from so long ago and that I have longed for so long. When I gently caress your forehead and ever so lightly run my fingers through your hair, you let out the softest little whimpers that let me know you are dreaming of me. When I hold you as you sleep, I know that I want to hold you forever.

Chapter 3

Bliss

I told you that I would lead you into bliss, so let me just say that ours was the most beautiful wedding ever! No, we did not have the most flashy, flamboyant, or fanciful venue. We did not spend exorbitant amounts of money on decorations. The men's tuxedos were rented, and the bridesmaids' dresses, while stunning, were not created by the most accomplished fashion designers. The music was provided by friends and family playing piano and acoustic guitar for the price of being able to be a part of our joyous celebration. We did not hire the finest tenors to perform an opera for our celebration; we simply enjoyed the vocals of those who knew us best. Why then, you may ask, do I say we had the most beautiful wedding ever?

From my perspective, this wedding was so beautiful because it was not about a wedding as much as it was about a marriage. The bride wore a splendid white dress with a medium-low cut neckline lined with a lace pattern of two vines and budding flowers coming together as one. The sleeves came to just past the wrist with the same lacy vine pattern circling down the bride's arms, giving the appearance of modesty entwined in delicacy and elegance. The total length of the dress came to the bride's feet and formed a small train in the back. The garment was tight at the waist and formed a pleated bell shape as it flowed to the ground. It had a silky look with a large bow just at the bottom of the lower back. A large white headpiece and veil adorned the head of the bride, which gave a halo effect and the imagery of an angelic being glowing before her witnesses.

The groom wore a white tuxedo with white bow tie and cummerbund. The jacket was white and tailed, giving a look that stood out from everyone else, yet it did not quite look complete until it was next to the flowing gown of the bride. Finishing the groom's ensemble was a pair of dazzling white shoes. The overall look of the bride and groom was brilliance and purity—a man and a woman coming together as God intended, clean and innocent.

This wedding day was probably much like most wedding days. Family and friends from out of town came to revel in the occasion, bringing with them those two oh-so-familiar gifts for the bride and groom: stress and frustration. The bride was with her people, performing the traditional pre-wedding rituals of applying make-up, styling and restyling her hair, being advised too much and listening to too little, and generally being put into a state commonly referred to as a "nervous wreck." In the midst of this frenzied activity, the bride was, however, able to escape this state of mind being thrust upon her. And just as the prophets of old would see coming events, Lisa could look ahead to a point later in that day. The bride was calm, and the only emotion welling up in her that day was joy.

The groom, I knew well: he was me. Therefore, I have no problem recounting how well-adjusted he was. I imagine I woke up that morning feeling like any other red-blooded American young man that was getting married that day. I was calm, cool, and collected. I had everything under control. This was the day I had been waiting for with eagerness and enthusiasm. I was about to accept the biggest responsibility of my life by leaving behind the "me" and taking on the "we." After this day, I would make no more life decisions alone. They would be made together with another: my wife.

It was almost time. The soft tracked music was playing in the sanctuary at our church as the guests began to arrive. Ushers were showing them to their seats as they talked in hushed tones. Their murmurs sounded like gentle ocean waves washing upon the shore of some secluded island beach. The sound guy was doing his last-minute checks while the pastor took a shot of Listerine in the foyer men's room. The bride was waiting at the front of the church, keeping the traditional measure of distance from the groom, who was at the back of the church. Oh yes. The groom (me) was ready for everything. Things were hoppin' back in the groom's area. Groomsmen were adjusting their bow ties, instructions were being given on how to stand for long periods of time without fainting (always keep one knee slightly bent), boutonnieres were being pinned to lapels, and I, the groom, had forgotten my underpants! No, I wasn't nervous. Not me. Thank goodness Gainesville was a small town because I had to make a quick trip home to retrieve the most important part of an all-white tuxedo! I did make it back on time, and now it was time.

The pastor stood at his podium, Bible open with a small sheet of paper containing matrimonial notes, keeping his place in 1 Corinthians 13. With a sober stoicism about him, he prepared to usher a young couple he had watched grow up in the youth section of pews at First Assembly into the newest and most mature phase of their lives. If you looked closely enough, you might even perceive a small tear of joy forming in the corner of his left eye as he reminisced over the years of watching these two grow from the children who would pass notes and find all the comedic blunders of a Sunday morning sermon to those teens who washed the altars with their tears at the after-service altar calls to the two betrothed who would soon stand before him, and under God, to give their vows of matrimony.

The minute hand on the clock made its last tick, and it found the hour hand ready and in position. It was time! As the music came up, the attendants quieted and turned their attention to the doors at the front of the church, which were now open and giving admittance to the bridal party. The bridesmaids joined their groomsmen and formed the bridal train to the stage, where they would separate and go to their respective areas—maids on the pastor's right and men on his left. The groom was already standing down in front of the altar.

The bride's father was not present for this moment in their lives. However, in lieu of Lisa's father walking her down the aisle and giving her away, we had worked out something different. Different would later become a descriptor of our entire lives, Lisa's and mine. Here is what happened. Lisa walked through the doors at the front of the church, and when I beheld her radiant beauty, everything in my life stopped. Time stood still, no one moved, sound ceased to travel through the air, light and shadows did not exist, my heartbeat became one eternal beat, and I even ceased to breathe. This was the moment of all moments for me—the moment of my bride, Lisa. Lisa's uncle Charles stepped up and extended his left arm for her to interlock her right arm through, and then he began walking her down the aisle. As Lisa and her uncle began their slow procession toward the altar, where I was standing, I began to slowly walk toward them. Just as the groom of the Old Testament would go to his betrothed when he had prepared a place for them, I was now walking to meet my bride and take her to the altar with me. We met in the middle of the church, where Lisa's uncle released her to me. We then proceeded, arm in arm, to stand before the pastor and proclaim our vows one to the other.

The ceremony had begun, music played, vows were spoken, and rings were exchanged. And then the words "you may kiss the bride" rang out through the sanctuary, followed by cheers and applause! Reverend James R. Jackson raised his hands, encompassing us between them, and extended them toward the assembly as if he was forming a shroud of covenant around us, this newlywed couple, Mr. and Mrs. Brad Llano.

The wedding was over, the marriage had begun, and everyone wanted to celebrate with this brand-new couple, the Llanos. We took our wedding photos then proceeded to the reception, where we received congratulatory hugs and handshakes. We had wedding cake and punch and all the traditional trappings of a hometown wedding. Lisa and I were all blushes and smiles as we were inducted into that new caste, the young married couples group. Say goodbye to the youth group.

Love Language

Learning a love language isn't the easiest thing to do, but it is probably one of the most rewarding. Saying the words "I love you" is only the beginning of the journey down that difficult road that leads to a beautiful destination. Along the way, we learn when to listen and when to speak. We are careful to try to understand those little nuances in each other's voice that indicate when we are happy, sad, apprehensive, scared, upset, pleased, comfortable, or just plain gushing with love for each other. We discover how to be patient and kind, especially when we want to be defensive and defend our points. We strive to find out what it is that soothes a frustrated tone or brings out a laugh in the midst of turmoil. We love with our eyes. We love with our thoughts. We love with our words and with the work we are willing to put in to help each other grow. We promote peace, and we long to embrace. We are romance's biggest advocate, and we find ways to never let an argument go unresolved. Lisa, I love you! Now I travel down that difficult road to my "beautiful" destination.

Chapter 4

What Now?

What were Lisa and Brad to become? What would life look like now that the two were one? A day of wedded bliss may have been behind us, but there was still a short drive to downtown Dallas where we had a reservation at the Doubletree Hotel. Yes, a day of wedded bliss had to be followed by the honeymoon.

Waking Up Thinking of You

I always wake up thinking of you, and that makes me very happy. I will have a good day because I will be thinking of you throughout it. I also love our talks. They continue to reveal how much we are meant for each other. You do help me every day. I only regret that we have missed so many days until now. They say "until death do us part." I LOVE YOU WITH NO UNTILS ATTACHED! To love, honor, and cherish…for richer or poorer, in sickness and in health, through thick and thin for all time. I make this vow to you!

Our honeymoon lasted two days and three nights, and the greater part of that glorious weekend will not be discussed in this book. I will tell you that we thoroughly enjoyed each other completely free from awkward tension or the newlywed jitters that some would say is a natural part of becoming husband and wife. The days were filled with fun activities such as breakfasts and lunches and movies or swimming at the pool with my father and stepmother. This is because they paid for our honeymoon, and what that meant to my father was that he got to plan the whole weekend. This was his thing. The evenings were for Lisa and me alone. The evenings were for passion, connection, and affection.

In spite of the all-controlling dad-meister, Lisa and I had a wonderful and most memorable honeymoon weekend. Our love, commitment, and dedication for each other had been consummated, and we were on our way.

With Solomon's Help

I have been feeling particularly sexual about you today, so I decided to go to God's Word on the subject. I was reading through Song of Songs when I came to the following quote: "You are all together beautiful, my darling; there is no flaw in you... You have stolen my heart, my sister, my bride; you have stolen my heart with one glance of your eyes; with one jewel of your necklace. How delightful is your love my sister, my bride! How much more pleasing is your love than wine, and the fragrance of your perfume than any spice! Your lips drop sweetness as the honeycomb, my bride; milk and honey are under your tongue (Song of Songs 4:7–10 LSV)." There is so much to the relationship we have. There are so many levels: attraction, affection, affirmation, sexuality, sensuality, submission (to God's will and to each other), friendship, partnership, and agreement. Once again, I end with "I love you!"

I woke up Monday morning back in Gainesville, in our little one-bedroom rented house. I looked over at Lisa, who was peacefully sleeping beside me. The early morning sun beaming in through our bedroom window gave her a radiant glow, and I lay there staring at her in quiet disbelief that this was all real. I had a wife, and I was the happiest man in the world! We found joy in every activity of the day and night; we were the happiest couple in the world. For us, it was heaven just picking out a comforter and pillow shams for the bedroom or setting up for our first home interior party or even going to the grocery store.

A Quickie

It's exactly what you think. A love thought jumps into my mind, and suddenly, I am flushed, discombobulated, excited, and wanting to hold and kiss you, stroke your hair, and whisper sweet nothings in your ear. It can happen anytime or anywhere, and I am helpless to do anything about it. My love for you, I now declare!

So "what now" was to be a life together. It was no longer a singular life for either of us but a partnership, a united front—us against the world. We still did what every new adult has to do: go to work, pay the bills, buy groceries, visit friends, and attend holiday gatherings. But now we planned all these things around us, not me.

Our first big test as newlyweds was to be our attendance at my side of our family's Thanksgiving get-together in Fort Worth, Texas. Remember, us against them! Every year, for as long as I can remember, my extended family would get together at my aunt Sandra's house in Fort Worth for Thanksgiving and at my aunt Beatie's house in Gainesville for Christmas. Shortly after Lisa and I were married, the summer came to an end, ushering in the autumn and winter festivities. Tactical planning was required here, and we were up to the task. We weighed our options, formed our plan, and made the consensual decision to plunge in headfirst, to hanging with the in-laws. Lisa, you go first!

Let me emphasize here that Lisa and I were true lovebirds. We truly believed there was nothing we could not do together. At this point, nothing in life scared us. Lisa was so excited to be on my arm for her first Thanksgiving with her new in-laws. What Lisa did not know was that this would be the first Thanksgiving that my aunts and uncles and great-aunts and great-uncles would even consider me an adult and not the keeper of their kids while they played cards and had interesting adult conversations. That's right. I had been graduated to the adult table with all the privileges and honors that came with the title of full-grown man. I suspect it's because this year, I brought something new to the table: my beautiful wife.

Now my family would never have been considered a quiet, subdued, or even laid-back group. The truth is that my family would most adequately be described as more eclectic and rowdy than that youth group I mentioned earlier. Lisa was not inexperienced in raucous family gatherings, but now she was meeting a brand-new family. Lisa was thrilled.

We arrived at the objective in Llano couple mode. We advanced, dug in, and became the new life of this traditional holiday assembly. All the while, we were hand in hand, never separated, one unit working in tandem. We beamed with delight as we withstood the countless interrogations and scrutiny of all those who had been married longer and wanted to impart that wise sage experience that came with the maturity they must surely have possessed after sustaining those long and fruitful marriages.

Lisa and I were the perfect team. We sat at the adult table, played their games, and laughed until we cried. However, what I remember being the best part of that day was when I took Lisa outside for a walk down to a little park and playground a few blocks from my aunt's house. The air was crisp and cool as we breathed in that beautiful autumn afternoon. You could hear the birds up in their trees, singing their own tunes of thanksgiving underneath an azure sky speckled with soft white clouds, which provided just enough shade to temper heaven's spotlight that seemed to always be shining on this young couple.

As we arrived at the park, we sat in the swings and talked. We sat on the see-saw and laughed as though we were those two children of earlier times. Then we stood under the shade of an oak tree, stared into each other's eyes, and kissed. This was not making out but rather the kiss of affirmation. We were happy.

A Little Love Note

We need heavy conversations now and then, but I prefer the fun giggling talks.

Following our first Thanksgiving was our first Christmas. We decided against the big family gathering for this one and to just have our own little living room celebration. I don't remember going all out on decorations for the house, but there was one thing we simply had to do. We had to find our own Christmas tree. Now this tree would not be bought at the local Walmart, nor would it be some superficial, artificial, three-part assembly, plastic-needle, scent-free tree. No, our first Llano family Christmas tree had to be real.

The details are a little fuzzy, but I will do my best to give a proper account of our first Llano family Christmas. I'm sure we all know that when searching for the perfect natural Christmas tree, we are looking for our grand firs, Douglas firs, Virginia pines, and white spruces. Lisa and I—in our infinite wisdom and out of pure necessity—went with an eastern red cedar. I say *necessity* because, as I recall, Lisa's mom had a boyfriend at the time who had access to a property that had eastern red cedars growing in abundance on it. As a newlywed couple, we still had to watch our finances, so cost was a factor. With the option we chose, the cost was one hacksaw, one afternoon, one tank of gas, and one person to hold the barbed wire fence up while the rest of us crawled through (I never questioned what "had access" meant).

I forget how many were in our party, but I do remember that Lisa and I made it onto the property (remember, unified front), where we located the perfect tree. I cut the tree down using the aforementioned hacksaw, and the boyfriend helped us secure it to his vehicle for transport back to our domicile. This was where we realized that the traditional artificial tree stand we had borrowed from Lisa's mother would not support a real six-foot eastern red cedar. I made a quick trip to my carport, where I had a metal bucket. Then it was off to the railroad track where I filled the bucket with stones for weight. I returned home, emptied the bucket, and placed the tree into the bucket. And while Lisa held the tree in place, I filled the bucket back up with the stones. Together, we moved the tree into our living room and added water. We set our ornaments, wrapped our tinsel, and we were set.

When Christmas Day arrived, it felt magical to wake up in my own home next to my wife, Mr. Llano. I was waiting for Mrs. Llano to wake up so we could go together into our living room and open presents. There were two presents under our tree: one from my wife to me and one from me to my wife. We had each gotten a bottle of cologne for the other. Lisa (in the red dress she had worn on the night of our engagement) and I (in my long terrycloth robe) put on the fragrances we had purchased for each other. We sat under our tree in a long warm embrace, savoring every second of this, our first Christmas.

A Gas Station Rose

Upon first inspection, one might surmise that the gas station rose is just an inexpensive sidetrack around taking the time and investing the effort to find the "reputable" florist who would select the finest and freshest of roses. The florist would then hand-deliver to the front door of one's lover, showing just how much thought, consideration, and love went into this endearing gift.

On further inspection, we see that the gas station rose is the truest gauge of the intent of the gifter to his lover. The gas station rose says, "It is not about the money but the desire to express love even in the tiniest of gestures." It says, "It is not the size of the gift but the fact that he feels compelled to give gifts, as if to show his courting nature." The gas station rose says, "Even at the end of a hard day's work, while filling up the tank of his motorcycle, he can't help but go into the gas station with giddy pleasure to buy something—anything—for the one he loves." He can't pass by any opportunity, no matter how small, to show his feelings for his lover.

Chapter 5

THE DIRT ROAD

The road that Lisa and Brad were on had been paved with childhood fascination, teenage infatuation, and friendship that carried them through the ups and downs of life in a small country town. Their road had been paved with the curiosity that revealed a budding new emotion. That emotion was love. They had, thus far, survived those little jealousies and insecurities that always seem to accompany that awkward time of dating.

The pavement of their road had a base foundation, which was love. This was probably the most important part of the road Lisa and Brad were on. This foundation would later carry and sustain them far more than either of them ever imagined.

On this paved road, Lisa and Brad began a dream. They dreamed of becoming a youth pastor and a youth pastor's wife, of owning their own home and filling it with their children who would one day grow up, marry, and produce their own children: our grandchildren. Lisa and Brad dreamed of working together in life and retiring as a happy old couple with nothing but wonderful memories of holidays shared by the family they had created. They saw a world full of opportunity and filled with love. Lisa and Brad only saw the silver lining but never the dark clouds the lining shone through. Those clouds were beginning to form.

I Love You As

Sometimes we say, "I love you beyond words." Let me attempt to tell you how I love you with words. After all, words are what we have to work with, so let me try to put them to work.

I love you as the snowy mountain pass loves the first rays of sunshine come the thawing spring.

I love you as the thirsty blades of grass in the meadow love the first drops of an April shower.

I love you as the tallest oak loves the nourishing soil that surrounds its roots.

I love you as the eagle loves the wind that supports its wings in flight.

I love you as the sands of the ocean floor love the waves that form its contours.

I love you as the earth itself loves the sun that gives warmth in the cold of space.

I love you as the tides of the sea love the moon that affects them so.

I love you, Lisa, as a man created for a woman with a heart that beats for her alone, the one who holds his heart with gentle caress and passionate kiss. I love you beyond myself with all the words I can find.

At this point, I need to catch you up on some backstory. When I was a senior in high school, my father made a deal with me. He said, "Brad, I'll make a deal with you. If you will go to college, study, and make decent grades, I will pay for your tuition and books." I took the deal even though, at the time, I didn't particularly know what I would go to college for. By the time Lisa and I were preparing to be married, I had already received my associate degree and was attending North Texas State University, where I was working on a bachelor's degree in business. I was majoring in business because after finishing an associate degree in "the basics," I was still unsure of what it was I was supposed to be doing in college. My dad knew—business!

Back to the dreams of Lisa and Brad. It all started to make sense now. I told my father that when Lisa and I got married, I wanted to take a semester off and that I was thinking about leaving the business program and enrolling in a Bible college in order to get a degree in ministry. I told my father, with all the enthusiasm of a young Thomas Edison who had just invented the light bulb, about wanting to become a youth pastor and work hand in hand with my wife in the ministry. I told him how we felt called to a ministry working with youth and how he would be part of that ministry by financing my degree and that I finally, really, felt clear about, and focused on going to college. Yes, it all made sense now!

What was my father's response? "Well done, my son. I am so proud of you. You have obviously put a lot of thought and consideration into this decision, especially as you are about to enter into one of the most important roles a man has in this life—being a husband. I made a deal with you, and you still have my support." This was NOT his response! My father instantly came back with his dissatisfaction at my even wanting to get married at this point. He considered my taking a semester off to regroup and look into a degree plan at an accredited Bible college as my resignation from college altogether. I was told that I should finish a business degree from the college I was already enrolled in and not get married, or he would not pay for my education any longer. I couldn't believe it. My dad was reneging on the deal that he had made.

All of a sudden, the paved road that Lisa and I traveled had some gravel on it. That conversation with my father settled it. I did leave the business program at North Texas State. I did marry Lisa, and my father harbored resentment toward me from that day forward. Of course, as a newlywed couple, we had to watch our finances. Now that my father's financial assistance was pulled, we couldn't afford to just pick up and move to a new town, find housing, and put me back in school. The ministry would have to wait.

So a unified front, right? I wish I could say that I never made mistakes, that I always clearly saw the path that should be followed and followed it. I wish I could say that, at least, I always followed my own advice. The truth is, I often made mistakes, rarely saw the clear path, and as far as my own advice goes, I was usually my own worst enemy. In an attempt to shelter my beloved Lisa from what I perceived as an unfair attack against our marriage from my father,

I kept his remarks to myself. This was one of the first chips in our unity, and I was the one who inadvertently put it there. In what I thought was an act of protection, I kept information from my wife that she needed in order to rally to my side so we could act together, in unison, against any foe.

Our beautifully paved road would get rougher and bumpier as the weeks and months went on. The smooth shoulders of our road began to erode with insecurities, frustrations, and jealousies. Another chip in our unity was the one thing I don't recall being covered in our premarriage counseling: premarriage baggage. Both Lisa and I had traumatic events in our respective pasts (some known and some at the subconscious level) that would shape our psyches for years to come. We were so in love and so desirous of that wedded bliss that we both knew should be ours. So we packed our bags, threw them in the proverbial trunk, and drove them right into our marriage, not thinking they would ever come out of that trunk to harm us.

Once the seed of insecurity took root within Lisa, it began to manifest itself as jealousy. I tried to reassure and comfort, but I did not know how to get to the root of what was starting to turn our paved road into a dirt road. I am not even sure that I knew I needed to get to the root of anything. I still firmly held to the phrase "I love you, and that love will last forever." Here, I must pause and say that this was the most prophetic thing I have ever said, felt, believed, professed, proclaimed, pondered, or put into action in my life. That statement has held true from that time right up to the very moment you are reading the words on this page. The thing is, that phrase alone, as true as it was (and still is), was not enough to keep our new magnificently paved road from starting to crumble.

There is much work to be done if two people are to success-fully cultivate a lifelong partnership of trust, adoration, affection, consideration, and commitment. This is called covenant. Love's true meaning encapsulates all things necessary to form, bind, and honor a lasting covenant. Unfortunately, we don't always understand the true and full meaning of love (I will come back to that later).

I mentioned earlier that Lisa and I toted a lot of baggage into our newly formed covenant. When I declared my vows to Lisa on our wedding day, I did not say that I would drag my tote of past traumas (which would remain unexplained), insecurities, hurts, unrealistic expectations, and mental instabilities into our new covenant. Lisa did not include these things in her vows either. I know what you're thinking: *No one says that when declaring their wedding day vows.* True. However, when vows are exchanged, we say we will honor, meaning to never disgrace and always do our best to lift up each other. We say we will cherish, meaning to hold dear and to cultivate, not to overlook issues of the heart and mind but to be a partner in dealing with those issues. These two words, *honor* and *cherish*, are preceded by the word *love*.

We tend to think these three words are separate (to love, honor, and cherish) when, in fact, the latter two are actually descriptors of the first. These vows we proclaim are given some non-limitations: "For better or worse, in sickness and in health, for richer or poorer, until death do us part." This means that the individual lives being bound here are bringing all their cheerfulness, sadness, humor, life experiences, brokenness, assuredness, security, insecurity, weakness, and strength (their baggage, good or bad) into this union, this covenant. These individual lives become one mutual life of commitment and understanding.

Lisa and I had not learned all this yet. For us, there was no sordid past because we only knew the moment we were in and the dreams of what was to come. We were not prepared for anything less than that perfectly paved road of our dreams. We knew that we could love each other enough to make those dreams come true; we just did not know the full extent of what love was. What we deemed normal childhood lives were broken homes. Our examples of family life were far from what we now thought would be our life together as Mr. and Mrs. Prince Charming. We had never really experienced a thriving, nurturing, and unified home. We really only knew how to fend for ourselves. This was where the pavement crumbled and became something entirely different. This was how we began driving on a dirt road, but where did this road lead?

Therapy

When you tell me that you become anxious outside of your comfort zone, then tell me that you are comfortable with me. It is a sweeter sound to my ear than a favorite song of my youth. To know that I am that place where you feel most at ease makes me feel like I have found my purpose in this life. I always want to be that person that can stand next to you, know that you are beginning to feel nervous, and gently take your hand in mine, ever so lightly caressing to reassure you that you are not alone. When you can't catch your breath, I will gently kiss your cheek with the calming kiss that signifies, "I am here to help you breathe." When you feel the pressure of others' stares on you, I will put my reassuring arm around you, letting you know that you will never again have to bear the burden of insecurity, for those stares are on us. We will develop, heal, and weather any storm that comes our way together. Together, we are the best therapy for each other that money could not possibly buy. I love you in the way that the word love *conveys the most complete, compassionate, caring, rewarding, rich, and receiving emotion and covenant I can offer in the English language.*

Chapter 6

A Wooded Path

A forest can be both a beautiful and horrible place. The forest presents a canvas of greens and browns with dappled sunlight dancing across the gently swaying timbers, whose limbs are ever reaching toward the sky as if to say, "The sun shall not shine here." When the sun's rays do penetrate the wooded gauntlet, they provide that soft reassuring luminary, such as a nightlight provides for the young child afraid of the dark.

As your gaze falls on the forest floor, you might see a babbling brook whose waters shimmer, as if to provide yet another small source of light with which to navigate your path. Shadows are cast across the stones and fallen leaves appearing as wraiths dashing about and watching as you begin your journey into the forest.

The sounds and smells that surround you are captivating yet ominous. The creaking of the trees, as the breeze pushes and pulls them, sings a gentle lullaby while the chittering of woodland animals harmonize. The swishing crackle of critters darting through the thick underbrush as you walk along brings into existence a form of uneasy company. The smells of pine and wildflowers mix with that of decay and rotting wood. The winds from other places bring with them the aroma of herbs and fresh pools of water mingled with the scents of stagnant pools and death.

Thus far, I have told you about new beginnings, friendship, and companionship. I have described for you the joy of holy matrimony and the union of two young lovers. I have given you a picture of a newlywed couple's dreams. I have spoken about the paved road of two lovers' fantasy and how that fantasy began to be torn down by reality. I have mentioned the erosion of pavement into gravel and, eventually, dirt. I have asked the question of where the dirt road would lead, and now this must be addressed.

I confess that it is not an easy thing to remember, with any degree of accuracy, just how Lisa and I found ourselves on that dirt road. Everything had been so good. Then only five months after we said "I do," we found ourselves standing on that dirt road that led to a wooded path. Let me emphasize here that the wooded path only led into the forest and was not the forest itself.

On this wooded path, Lisa and I were still holding hands. We were still making our way forward in the life we were building, but our footing was becoming unstable. The ground we walked on was less than sturdy, and we began to stumble. Our love was secure, but we were beginning to realize that a marriage required more than "love." It required work.

Lisa and I began having small squabbles over meaningless things. This is what I remember thinking; however, the things we squabble over are never meaningless. Lisa began to show a jealousy that I could not or would not understand. I began to withdraw from intimacy and could not explain why. Lisa and I had entered into a marriage as damaged people; thus, our marriage was pre-damaged. This required work, but neither of us had been trained in this type of work.

In the coming months, as Lisa and I walked along the wooded path, I remember how Lisa spent much of her time crying, and I spent much of my time under the carport fiddling with worthless projects while separated from my wife, trying to avoid another argument. I realized that something serious was happening. I sought help from my family and friends, who, while heartbroken at our condition, had no problem with informing me that, "These things happen," "Sometimes marriages don't work out," "It sounds like you have done all you can do," "Maybe you should get a divorce," "What if you wait until you have a house and kids and still have problems? It would be worse to have to divorce at that point." Like I said, we were damaged before we ever got married.

Lisa and I went further and further down that wooded path trying to talk it out, cry it out, yell it out, and wait it out. Where did this path lead? It led to a forest! I would suggest a separation in order to work out our feelings. Lisa would take this as the beginning of the end. She did not feel as if I would stay, and why would she? I was talking about separations and working things out alone. How does that encourage a young bride whose only model of marriage was adultery, divorce, and a broken home? So now she thinks that is what is happening to her. I was oblivious.

As we neared the end of the path, my take on the situation was that Lisa was now anything but happy. I thought that I had tried to heal when all I did was tear down, and it was all happening so fast. There was no wisdom in me when I decided that if Lisa was unhappy and nothing I was doing could make her happy, I must be the wrong man for her. I could not be responsible for ruining the life of the one I loved. I finally suggested to Lisa the one thing I had never believed in: divorce.

The Heart Attack

One day, when I was younger, I was walking in a mall. I was happy enough, and it was a pleasant outing. As I walked, I began to have trouble catching a full breath. I started to feel lightheaded, and my left arm began to ache. I wasn't sure why I was feeling this way; I hadn't been ill recently. Then I felt a sharp pain proceeding from my chest outward.

I sat down at the edge of a water fountain and tried to regain my composure. There were people walking past me, having conversations and joyfully shopping. The fountain that I was sitting by was flowing with life and the sound of soothing happiness. I was watching these people bustle and scurry through the mall while I listened to the peaceful murmuring of the fountain beside me as it dawned on me that I was having a heart attack. How could this be? I was only in my thirties. I was healthy, energetic, and fit. I was incredulous! Still, it was happening. Slowly and with difficulty, I went to my car and made it back home. I called work and told them I would not be in that evening. I lay down on my bed and stayed there, not knowing if this would get better or worse. Finally, sleep came. The next day, I went to my doctor, who confirmed my fear. My heart was broken.

The heart's purpose is to sustain life. It does this by beating steadily and rhythmically in order to pump blood throughout the body, transporting what the body needs to stay alive. The heart's function is to love.

We talk about matters of the heart and the affairs of the heart. We say that we give our hearts in love. The emotions of the soul are felt in the heart. When two people fall in love, their hearts begin to sync. They begin to find a shared rhythm in order to beat as one. When this happens and the two hearts are working properly together, synchronous—rhythmically, adoringly, and strongly encouraging, caring for, and supporting each other—then the two hearts that beat as one sustain love. What happens when love has a heart attack, when the two hearts get out of sync? Love suffers. Confusion and pain invade the beautiful flowing meadow of love, turning it into a battlefield. Misunderstanding and doubt war against the two hearts that had become one.

When the dust settles, two hearts are broken and scarred. Love has had a heart attack!

Remember my heart attack at the mall? "What happened after that?" you may ask. Two things happened:

1. *God gave me an immediate healing. I had had an irregular heartbeat that had led to a minor coronary. God gave me a regular heartbeat.*
2. *God gave me a healing over time. Slowly, my heart got stronger and stronger. I have never had another heart attack.*

Lisa, our hearts fell in sync a long time ago. They developed a steady, rhythmic beat that became one heart. I believe that our love was and is one of the strongest and most enduring loves known. It has been put into the fire, dragged through the desert, hurled off a cliff, and cast into the depths of the sea. Our hearts have been broken but not destroyed. Life still pumps through the body of our love. These two hearts that God created for us have gone through an immediate and miraculous healing. God reunited us! Our hearts are also going through a healing over time.

The only way this makes sense to me is that we will become stronger and stronger over time, and we will never have another heart attack again.

My love for you is patient. I will give you every day that God allows me to live so that your heart may be fully healed. I love you during the times of delight and prosperity, and I love you when the storms rage around us. I love you more than myself. We have survived the heart attack.

I love you.

Chapter 7

Into the Forest

The paved road was gone. The dirt road had terminated, and the wooded path was nothing more than a goat trail surrounded by briars and thistles. The brilliance of the sun was choked out by the timbers and foliage of the forest, leaving cold shadows to prevail as if it was in mourning for the two lovers. The air was thick and rancid. The perfume of summer and fall had faded, and the fermenting cold of winter set in.

The two young lovers—that newlywed couple, Lisa and Brad—walked into the forest, still trying to hold hands. However, somewhere along the way, they lost their grip. As they walked deeper and deeper into that foreboding place, they walked farther and farther apart until, at last, they couldn't even see each other anymore.

My father told me that one of his close friends was an attorney. My father told me that his friend would help me with the divorce and that the cost would be minimal. My father and his attorney friend were very wrong about the cost. That divorce cost me everything; it cost Lisa everything. The cost of that divorce was our hopes, our dreams, our ministry, and our family. It cost us our happiness. It cost me my wife and Lisa her husband. I would never be the same, nor would she. Life, as we knew it (or, rather, wanted to know it), ended that day.

It was June 1, 1989. The sky was overcast, as though it knew this was a somber occasion. The air was heavy and difficult to breathe in, foreshadowing the struggle that was to come. A listless breeze whispered a melancholy tune of doleful distress as it lightly passed by. I was waiting outside the Cooke County Courthouse for my father's lawyer friend, the one who was doing me this great service. My mind raced with a current of thoughts like the roaring rapids of some mighty rushing river. I could not collect a single one in the attempt to form any sort of cohesive sentence or phrase. I had a nervous energy, like that of electricity dancing across the high wires of a power plant, that would not allow me to be at ease. On the outside, I sat on the steps of the courthouse with a stony face, expressionless, exhibiting complete calmness. On the inside, I was exploding. I felt like I was Hiroshima, and "the bomb" had just been delivered.

The attorney arrived and walked inside the courthouse with me. He had his hand on my shoulder, as if suggesting he was there to comfort me in my time of need. I did not need him. I needed to turn around, leave that house of impending destruction, and drive as fast as I could back to Lisa. I needed to grab her and hold her in my arms, to tell her that I loved her and that everything would work out. I needed to tell Lisa that we were leaving the forest. We were sticking together, and it was us against the world!

I walked like a zombie with the attorney's hand on my shoulder. He wasn't comforting me. He was leading me like beef to the slaughterhouse. Why was I doing this? Oh yeah. I didn't want to ruin Lisa's life. I was not the right man for her, and we had made a mistake. Lisa wasn't happy, and I couldn't make her happy. I love her, I love her, I LOVE HER!

While all this was going on in my mind, I could see the attorney standing before the judge with open briefcase, giving documents and making gestures as the judge nodded his head in agreement. Then, all of a sudden, I heard the words: "Okay, it's done. We're all finished here." Wait, what just happened here? That was it? Was my marriage over? The words in the divorce decree pronounced my marriage dissolved, as if the covenant Lisa and I had entered into could just be dropped into a vat of solution and washed out of our lives like some stain on a piece of clothing.

As my dad's friend, the lawyer, got into his car to leave, he looked at me, smiled, and said, "Have a nice day." This was all wrong. Nothing felt right about what had just happened. I wanted to run back into the courthouse, grab whatever documents the judge had signed just moments before, and tear them to shreds and scream, "My marriage is not dissolved!" Instead, I stood there at the bottom of the courthouse steps, deaf and blind to everything around me, finally realizing that my marriage to Lisa was now legally over. I could almost see the ground beneath my feet transform to twig-covered earth and loose stone. From that earthen floor grew the twisted vines climbing through the trees that encompassed me. I could smell the pungency of stale air and dead leaves in my nostrils. Heavy and dark shadows descended upon me, and in an instant, the path of my life plunged deep into the darkened forest of which I had no compass to navigate through.

A Prayer for My Love

Lisa, I want to share with you a conversation I had one day with God. This is not a historical account or a letter about details. It is a letter about emotions.

I had heard the words "That is it, it's done," but I couldn't believe that, just like that, our marriage had ended. I stood on the sidewalk in front of the Cooke County Courthouse in a fog. In my mind, I wanted to run back into the courthouse and beg the judge to throw away the divorce papers he had just, moments before, so nonchalantly signed into the law that would hang so heavily around my neck for so many years to come.

I didn't run back into the courthouse. I slowly walked away in tears. What had I done?

I told myself that I would never be married again—that I would never love again. My heart was more than broken; it was mortally wounded.

Years later, I found myself walking down a wooded trail beside a gently flowing creek in Arlington, Texas. It was a beautiful spring afternoon. The air was crisp, and there was a feeling of freshness all around. But I was not happy. This was the place I would come to for solitude. This was the place where I thought I could, at least momentarily, escape the turmoil my life had become. I would think and reflect and ponder my existence. I would call on God in the cool of the garden, and on this day, that is exactly what I did.

I thought back to my words: "I will never love again." I began to cry as I implored God, "Please, please, please, dear Heavenly Father, send me the woman who will love me as much as I love her!" I had realized that my heart did want to love, but I had given the love of my life away. I had nothing left but to ask God for a second chance, to give me the woman whose love I could not throw away.

For a moment that seemed like an eternity, I heard nothing but the light rustling of the leaves on the trees as the wind gently passed through them. I slowly began to hear the soft ripple of the water flowing in the creek beside me. Then I heard God say, "I have sent you what you have asked for." My heart leapt and began to warm. Joy began to rise within my spirit. God heard me and answered.

For Lisa, the forest must have been filled with confusion and hopelessness. The stifling air that choked her lungs was laced with betrayal. The mossy ground and slippery rocks were all that was left of her hopes and dreams. Those once so cherished visions of a home and children were now a stumbling block to her. When Lisa looked into that dark and wretched forest, all she could see was despair. The woodland creatures chittered and growled their taunting tunes of pain and agony. The winds howled through the trees like banshees singing their woeful dirge. What was this poor, fragile, newly divorced nineteen-year-old girl to do?

So as the months went on, I found myself more and more lost. Nothing made sense to me. I found myself in a small one-bedroom apartment on the outskirts of town. I felt dead inside, and I did not know how I was supposed to live after the divorce. My world had been wrapped up in taking care of Lisa, and now I had put her away. I felt like she would hate me forever, and that was the worst feeling I had ever known. I felt like her family, whom I had grown up with because of my friendship with her cousin Bryan, now hated me. It felt like the eyes of the entire town were on me. Their scrutiny was palpable. I truly felt like the bad guy, and I thought I was able to be that in order to give Lisa a chance at a happier life—a life with the one who was truly right for her. I knew nothing.

There is no tasteful way to say what happened next. In order to avoid bringing shame on those who were not at fault, I will state for the record that I was totally at fault in every failed relationship that passed through my life since Lisa. Not long after the divorce, I met a girl who went to the community college across the road from my apartment. Without getting mottled in the details, I must tell you that Prince Charming fell from his white steed during this time. As a result of my lack of self-control and good judgment, she became pregnant, which shot the final bolt into the coffin that was once my marriage. It was a small town, and when Lisa heard about the pregnancy, it solidified, in her mind, the belief that she would never be with me again—that she would not have the family she wanted with me. The news tore her dream to shreds.

I Think I Know

I think I know what I need to do. I have told you that I cannot say that I didn't love you. I have told you that I cannot say that I wanted our marriage to end. I have told you that I wanted what was best for you. The thing is, only I can understand or make sense of those statements.

I have said that I understood what you went through, but that's simply not the case. I accepted and agreed with what I thought you must have been going through (but that is not the same thing). I have told you that I did all I could, but that is not true. I could have and should have waited. I should have endured. I should have stayed, until death would we part. I was supposed to pray with you and read God's Word with you. I was supposed to protect you from all harm, including the harm done to your heart.

I have told you that I never cheated on you, but the fact that I listened to anyone other than God, you, and my own heart in the matter of divorce did certainly cheat us out of our marriage, our home, and the children we would have raised there. I ended our family before it ever had a chance to live.

We read in Mark, "But at the beginning of creation God made them male and female. For this reason, a man will leave his father and mother and be united to his wife, and the two will become one flesh.

So, they are no longer two, but one. Therefore, what God has joined together, let man not separate… Anyone who divorces his wife and marries another woman commits adultery against her. And if she divorces her husband and marries another man, she commits adultery" (Mark 10:6–9, 11–12).

Lisa, I confess to you that I alone did separate what God joined. I was the culprit in this unrighteous act. I confess to you that every relationship I had with any woman after our marriage, to whatever degree that relationship might have been, was an adulterous act against you and a sin against my Heavenly Father and the Holy Spirit. The marriage I entered into after our divorce, even though it was years later, should not have happened, and I am only now fully able to see that. I have been wrong about everything. I have only allowed myself to see things through the tinted lens of my own reality.

I did want out of our marriage in 1989 because I was too short-sighted to see that things could, and surely would, get better. I allowed my own desire for happiness to override the true joy our marriage would have produced over a lifetime of going through and overcoming trials and tribulations that are a part of every righteous act, marriage being one of the greatest.

Lisa, I confess my guilt under a veil of shame. The mistake was mine, and you were blameless. I failed to cherish that wonderful gift that God gave me, and I plunged you into a lifetime of misery. Now all I can do is ask you to forgive me. I do love you, and I will be yours if you will still have me.

After the decision was made not to abort this new life that was being formed (and there was never any argument about that), other decisions had to be made. Was I to remarry in order to father this child? I had been raised to believe that that was the honorable thing to do. Were we to give the baby up for adoption? We did not have the relationship that would sustain a marriage, and I knew that I did not love her. One day, as we talked over all our options, it happened; she told me that she loved me. Whatever else I had become by this point, I was, at least, honest. I told her that I could not marry her because I did not love her.

One evening during this period, I left my apartment and walked across the road out behind the college where there was a large field. It had been raining. The sky above knew that on this evening, I would not cry, so the sky cried for me. The sky wept down onto that field and moaned its peals of thunder as I, laboring, trudged out into the middle of that soupy terrain. The mud seemed to grab at my ankles, as if it were attempting to pull me to my knees. The winds whipped the tears of the heavens into my eyes as I dragged myself onward to the middle of that field—the place where I would, for the first time, scream at God.

This was a real place in the metaphorical forest I was in. I was not trapped; I was pushing forward. I was going deeper and deeper into a place where my heart did not belong. I was breaking down.

The sinews in my legs burned with each agonizing step. My heart was beating hard within my chest, as though it was trying to leap from my body and leave this horrible place where love was stifled and joy dampened. I fell to my knees, sinking into the sloppy muck below me with arms raised toward heaven, fists clenched, and head thrown back. I knew not what to do, what to say, what to ask, or how to receive. I simply screamed into the howling winds as the stinging rivulets of rain bit into my skin. My wails created the harshest of harmonies for the squalling winds. I felt insane.

That evening, God held me in His arms. He calmed the storm, and He calmed my spirit. I went home, cleaned up, and went to bed. With each new dawn, the future would arrive as the present, regardless of my mental state.

We did not marry; I could not. We did not raise the child together; she would not. She knew that I didn't love her, but more to the point, she knew why I didn't love her. She knew that my heart belonged to Lisa, and that was the end for her. She moved back home to her mother, declared "father unknown" when the baby was born, and moved on with her life without me.

Now I felt the weight of what I would carry as the destruction of not one but two lives!

Chapter 8

Not on Track

If you were to ask me, "What is your nature?" I would have to inform you that, from the earliest times, it was that of the comedian. My main goal in life has always been to make people laugh.

For nearly a year after the divorce, I just didn't know what to do. I wanted to see Lisa, but I knew that would be like adding salt to an open wound for her. Still, we would run into each other, and this was taking its toll on Lisa. My emotions were all over the place, and I was steadily losing my perspective on why I had divorced my wife. My thoughts were anything but coherent. I was building a facade. On the outside, I was starting to appear as I used to: smiling, laughing, making others laugh. On the inside, I was a shipwreck of a person, trying to salvage anything that might keep me afloat in the turbulent waters of my heart and mind.

Remember, this was a small country town. The rumor mill had started working overtime to produce a level of misinformation that would stagger the best intelligence operatives. Lisa's family, my church family, and even mutual friends of ours were voicing their imaginations of the infidelities I must have committed prior to our divorce. They were giving their unsolicited testimonials of fresh new romantic entanglements I was engaged in while still in the wake of the destruction of our marriage. The spies I never hired were making their reports to me on Lisa's whereabouts and how she had so much more than gotten over me and moved on. It was intolerable and becoming unbearable.

One sunny Saturday afternoon, I was at the local Piggly Wiggly grocery store in order to get some necessities. I was out for the usual products: bread, butter, milk, eggs, sandwich meat, and the one thing I was really in the mood for on that particular Saturday afternoon, Blue Bell chocolate chip ice cream. It was a low-traffic time when I arrived at the store, so I parked in the middle of the lot, went inside, and began the shopping experience.

I found everything on my list, proceeded to the checkout counter, paid the agreed-upon purchase amount, then headed to the parking lot. I was midway across the parking lot between the grocery store and my car, a bag of groceries in each arm, when I heard the familiar sound of a 1979 Oldsmobile Cutlass. It was Lisa's car, and Lisa was driving it. I looked to my right to confirm what my ears already knew. Lisa was turning into the parking lot. In the preceding paragraphs, I have described my mental state. Now let me add to that description the fact that I was an idiot. I saw Lisa, smiled, and lifted my right arm with groceries, signifying that I was waving hello. That's when I heard it. The engine in Lisa's '79 Olds Cutlass revved up. She was accelerating! I could actually see her eyes narrow as she stepped on the gas pedal. I threw the groceries, dove out of the way of the car, and looked over my shoulder to witness my ice cream falling to the ground and producing the perfect spatter as it crashed upon the pavement.

Yes, this can be an amusing piece of the narrative. However, it was actually one of the last events that would make me realize I needed to leave Gainesville, Texas.

Assurance

Here goes. This may not exactly have the "love note" flavor you have become accustomed to from me, but it is important that you have this as a kind of reference material to return to and read as often as you need.

You asked me a question with tears in your eyes. The look on your face was a look that said you already knew what the answer would be. The thesis of this question had haunted you for decades, yet you could never shake the thought that you knew very well what the answer was.

Life had been thrown so far out of focus those many, many years ago that no life going forward could possibly ever be in focus again. Even though you have experienced moments of joy throughout your life, the overriding emotion has been torment. The question, the answer, the unknown?

When our life together separated, a whirlwind of reasons, whys, and wherefores surrounded us, and no clarity was to be found. But it always boiled down to that one question.

Were you unfaithful in our marriage? Had you wanted someone other than me? Was I not enough? These are just three versions of the same question: the QUESTION.

In your mind, you knew the answer must be yes. It was the only thing that could separate us in your mind. You have spent your whole life trying to reconcile that question and that answer.

My answer? NO! *I have always, and always will love you! I am so, so very sorry that you have lived with this for so long. I love you always and forever.*

I am certain that the action I took in 1989 can only fully be understood by me. It is worth noting that my life was thrown far, far out of focus also at that point. I was never unfaithful to you, Lisa. I cherished you and our marriage above all earthly things, even if I failed in it.

I have always loved you, Lisa. I will always love you, Lisa. You have always been with me, and I have only been unfaithful to the relationships I have had outside of us since us. I also believe that your heart knew this.

Chapter 9

ESCAPE TO ARLINGTON

So there was one more crucial piece of the equation that led to my departure from Gainesville, Texas, my hometown. One Sunday, I had gone to church, where I would sit in the back in order to avoid the accusatory stairs from my beloved church family and to facilitate an easy getaway after the service. Lisa was not there on this particular Sunday, but her mother, Donna, was. I decided that I should approach Donna after church so I could express my heartfelt concern for Lisa's well-being. I did just that. Donna was less than enthusiastic to speak with me, the bringer of desolation upon her daughter, about anything, especially about my concern for her divorced daughter's well-being. However, she did condescend to give me an audience.

I had actually spent the entire church service hour preparing and rehearsing, in my mind, exactly what I wanted to convey to Lisa's mother. I wanted to articulate how I never meant to hurt her daughter and how much I still cared about Lisa's happiness. I wanted to give my sincere apology to Donna, the mother of my ex-wife.

Out around the side of the church, when I stood before Donna (who was once my Sunday school teacher, my girlfriend's mother, and my mother-in-law), I felt the full weight of her disappointment. I looked into her eyes, and I saw no warmth in them for me. Donna returned my gaze with judgment and anger. I do not know if she ever forgave me, but there was no forgiveness that day. As I said, I had prepared myself for what I was about to say. Then I opened my mouth, and out came nothing but a barrage of questions. How was Lisa? What was she doing? Would it be okay if I called her? Do you think she wants to talk to me? Do you think she will forgive me? Would you talk to her for me? And so on and so on.

Donna let me empty my extensive tote of questions. She then informed me that Lisa had met someone, a man of God. Donna told me how this was important because Lisa had decided that she would not even date someone new unless he was a believer (as if I had not been). Donna observed that Lisa was doing fine. She briefed me on Lisa's painful recovery from our divorce and clued me in that she had moved on. Basically, what Donna was saying was "don't concern yourself with how Lisa is or what she is doing." It was not okay to call Lisa, and she did not want to talk to me. She had forgiven me and moved on, and Donna did not need to talk to her about me. This was the first time I thought that perhaps I had actually been right when I decided to divorce Lisa. I felt sick!

I Honestly Love You

> *Maybe I hang around here a little more than I should*
> *We both know I got somewhere else to go*
> *But I got something to tell you that I never thought I would*
> *But I believe you really ought to know*
> *I love you*
> *I honestly love you*
> *You don't have to answer, I see it in your eyes*
> *Maybe, it's better left unsaid*
> *This is pure and simple, and you must realize*
> *That it's coming from my heart, and not my head*
> *I love you*
> *I honestly love you*
> *I'm not trying to make you feel uncomfortable*
> *I'm not trying to make you anything at all*
> *But this feeling doesn't come along every day*
> *And I shouldn't blow my chance*
> *When I've got the chance to say*
> *I love you*
> *I love you*

I honestly love you
If we both were born in another place in time
This moment might be ending with a kiss
There you are with yours and here I am with mine
So, I guess we'll just be leaving it at this
I love you
I honestly love you
I honestly love you

(Source: Musixmatch, Songwriters: Jeff Barry / Peter W. Allen, "I Love You, I Honestly Love You" lyrics Woolnough Music, Jeff Barry Int., Irving Music Inc., Woolnough Music Inc.)

These are the lyrics to the popular song by Olivia Newton-John. I use this reference not as a comparison of our story but as a picture of true love and the power it holds.

In the very first verse of the song, we are given the sense that this is a love that will not be fulfilled. However, the love that our artist sings of is so true, dedicated, and honest that she has to declare it! She has to let the object of her love know.

Throughout the song and even to the end, we hear images of impossibility, of futility, of all the weight that sadness can weigh on a person when a dream cannot come true. But I am not speaking of dreams here. I am speaking of love in my own way, declaring my love for you, Lisa. The singer lets us know that these three simple and pure words, when uttered in honesty, override—no, overrule—all the logic and reasoning of the head. These three words overcome all the awkward and uncomfortable feelings that life has instilled in us. These three words: "I love you." I honestly love you.

I believe that these three simple, sure, and sincere words are the most powerful words in any language ever uttered by man, mankind, and even the Creator God toward His creation. "I love you" is a phrase not to be given or taken lightly.

When Olivia Newton-John sings this song, she conveys the idea that you need not respond, you need not react. There is no condition attached. I just have, right now, the opportunity to say "I love you" with a pure and honest love. And if I let this moment pass, I will regret it for the rest of my life.

She makes it clear that the only reason she is able to proclaim her love in the face of calamity is because this isn't that casual love we hear so often in everyday life. She says, "I love you. I honestly love you."

Lisa, I love you. I love you. I honestly love you!

What I should have done after Donna's rendition of the way things were was call Lisa and clarify. My heart needed to know, to hear it from her, but my head took Donna at her word. I remember thinking, *Why would Donna tell me something that wasn't true?* So I didn't call. I didn't get it straight from Lisa, and I began making plans for a move.

About this time, my friend Mike was having his own crisis of conscience and was preparing to leave for Arlington, Texas, where he would work on his bachelor's degree. I already had my associate degree in nothing, so I decided that completing a bachelor's degree in nothing would accommodate me in leaving this place, where the nimbus of depression was forming larger and larger over my head. I began seeking out Mike's knowledge of how to get to UT Arlington on very little money. While he pointed me in the direction of grants for tuition and housing, Mike would also make inquiries as to what my plans were, what my major was going to be, and so on. My response was simply that I needed to leave that small country town. To which Mike responded, "Oh, you're escaping."

Lisa and Brad had walked into a forest still clinging to each other. Then, in the darkness and confusing shadows of that forest, they were separated. Now they were about to be completely lost.

Mike and I made the move to Arlington, Texas, in September of 1990. Little did I know how that move would change my life. What I thought would help me heal most certainly did not have that effect. There was no way I could have been prepared for the next thirty-two years without Lisa.

Chapter 10

Insomnia

Lisa and Brad, wife and husband no more—the epitaph on the tombstone planted near an empty grave in the middle of the forest that seemed to have swallowed up young love. The marriage had died, but no bodies had been placed in that grave because their love was not dead yet, I suspect.

It was now the fall semester at UT Arlington, where I was enrolled as a physical education major with a minor in English, a junior in college. This was a busy degree plan that offered all the challenges and rewards that should have occupied my mind and distracted my heart. My mind was definitely occupied, but not with degree plans or scholarly thoughts. My heart would not be distracted so easily; it's singular purpose was Lisa. This institution of higher education was simply a new location for my heart and mind to agree on one thing: I still needed Lisa.

I began to bury my nose in my books. I would study my pain away. So here I was, as I said earlier—a jovial and happy college student on the outside but a remorseful, regretful, and rueful young man on the inside. I would go to all my classes, take all my notes, engage in the multitudinous study groups, pull all-nighters, and write the stifling number of papers each professor required in order to validate their existence. But what about my existence? This question began to take its toll on me as I would ponder it every night.

At the end of every school day, I still had my thoughts to contend with. I would lie in my bunk bed back at the dorm and think and think and think. I would finally close my eyes, then fifteen or perhaps thirty minutes later, I would rouse to beams of sunlight invading my small dorm room, heralding the new day, which just seemed to go on and on for me. I began falling asleep in the middle of the day during the most stimulating of lectures. I would wake up to those familiar stares from classmates that begged the question: "What were you dreaming?" I'll tell you what I was dreaming. I was dreaming of Lisa. She appeared just as I remembered her from one of her senior class pictures, with big eighties hair and wearing a fur coat. She would be walking toward me with neither smile nor frown on her face; she was neutral but advancing in my direction. I would have this dream, with variations, many times over the next thirty-one years. I was an insomniac.

I tried very hard to blend in, have fun, and go back to being the carefree guy I used to be. I was not the guy I used to be. After my second semester at UT Arlington, I realized that my grade point average was falling. I knew that I was eventually going to lose my grant money, so I found a job at a local video store. I was still in the dorm, and now I had a little gas and food money. I tried to have casual relationships with some of the girls on campus, thinking that might bring a sense of "normalcy." But nothing was normal, and no relationship went very far at all. It was always some laughs, a little romance, insomnia, Lisa, then the inevitable depression.

Dreams

You have been a lifetime of dreams for me. We would be together, all would be forgiven. We would make love and plan our future together while we held each other in the afterglow of the preceding ecstasy. Then I would wake up, and all was lost, and the worst part was that I had to go through that alone. Who could I share it with? I have lived a life of being devastated over and over until now. Now it all makes sense, and don't anyone dare pinch me because if I'm not awake and this is only a dream, I will gladly stay asleep forever! I love you so, so, so very much, and I look forward to every minute I can have with you until death do us part (except I don't believe we ever will really part).

Chapter 11

A Phone Call from Arlington

It was February of 1992. I was turning twenty-five, and life was nothing like I thought it would be at the beginning of my midtwenties.

I had restarted a college career. I worked at a video store in an unfamiliar town. I was surviving on candy bars and ramen noodles. I had reinvented myself as a chronic insomniac, and people were beginning to notice that something was wrong with me. What was wrong with me?

Not quite three years earlier, I had divorced my wife, Lisa—the first, best, and only true love of my life. I had felt so inadequate that I had convinced myself that her life would be ruined if I stayed in it. I did the unthinkable.

From the day our divorce was declared "final," I began a slow descent into the nonsense that would become my life. Everything I was or would have been, had I remained with my wife, was everything I could never be without her.

March of 1992 was now here. Dana Carter is a name I will never forget. It was the name of the video store manager. This woman had the discernment to realize that I was deteriorating. She knew the basic facts of my situation, and she instructed me to address the issue. Why she cared was beyond me, but what she said rang true.

After several days of introspection and pondering the outcome of my life if I did nothing and simply carried on as I had been, I decided to make a phone call. This was a difficult thing to do. In 1992, there were no unlimited calling plans. You had to pay for every phone call. I also had no idea what number to call. All I knew was WHO I had to call: my ex-wife.

What was on my mind? Reconciliation! I first called Lisa's mother and explained my intentions, then I asked for Lisa's phone number. After the deafening silence that followed, Donna told me that Lisa lived in Kansas City, Missouri, and gave me her long-distance number. This was the next obstacle.

How would I—a starving, struggling, part-time-working college student—be able to afford a phone call to Missouri long enough to persuade the one person who literally had every reason in the world to answer my call just so she could hang it up?

I asked my store manager for permission to use her office and office phone for one hour in order to make my best effort to bring the only woman who could save my life back to me. Dana gave her consent, her phone, and her office for one hour. Her last words as she shut the office door were "good luck."

I will leave this note unfinished for now. I assure you that all will be made clear in the end. So I made the call, but Lisa did not answer. I had to leave a message. This would not suffice! Now I had to beg, grovel, implore, do whatever it took to get an extension on the phone privilege so generously offered by my store manager. When I asked, Dana graciously and so empathetically placed her hand on my shoulder as she reassured me that I would have every opportunity she could provide for me to speak with Lisa.

I waited for what seemed like an eternity. I then reentered the manager's office, took a deep breath, and stared at the phone, remembering the words Dana had uttered earlier: "good luck." Was it luck that I needed? Was it resolve? Resolution? Did I need determination or just careless abandon? No, this was a leap of faith.

I had not been living these past three years. I had merely not physically died. I had been dead to everything in life that had ever meant anything to me. I didn't sleep. I didn't relate. I didn't want to be involved with anything. I was not going to church, and the few friends I had were finding it more and more difficult to carry on a normal conversation with me. I knew what the problem was: half of me was missing. I knew why that problem existed: I had put my wife away. No matter what the reasoning or how you justify it, separation is no solution.

I did not expect life to magically become perfect once I asked Lisa back into my life. I did not desire perfection. My desire was for restoration—the restoration of that young couple in love, who had been plunged into those stabbing thorns and choking vines of a broken union. I knew who was at fault: me.

I picked up the phone, dialed the number, then Lisa answered. As I recall, we used the entire hour I had been allotted as we talked about the past, present, and future of us. I was giving it my all with all the sincerity of genuine necessity that was within me. At one point, Lisa observed, "I don't think things could ever be the same." To which I replied, "I wouldn't want things to be the same." I told Lisa that our vows included for better or worse and that I felt like my decision to divorce and the three years that followed were the "worse." I told Lisa that I wanted to renew our marriage. There was a long pause. Then Lisa uttered in a hushed voice that almost seemed to be trembling with desperation, "That was good."

Could it be that this was the moment when all would be forgiven, as in the dream? Would this be the moment when we both realized that we were better at our worst moment together than we could ever be apart? Would Lisa come back and let me come back to her? Lisa informed me that she was engaged to be married and that the funeral, I mean wedding would take place in two months.

I made the call, and my life was changed forever. I did not win her back that night, but I did make her think.

Chapter 12

Letting Go

I was devastated, distraught, discouraged, wrecked, ruined, and broken. Now I had to let Lisa go. I had already destroyed her first marriage. How could I do anything to endanger her second chance at happiness? Even though I had already plotted a course on the map from Arlington to Kansas City, Missouri, factoring in the hours it would take, the cost of the fuel, and the weather forecast for the duration of the trip by motorcycle that I was already prepared to make, Lisa had said that she was remarrying.

I wanted to be that person who would make it to the church just in time to respond to the pastor's call for anyone who would object to this union with "Yes! I am here to object! That is my wife, and I want her back!" I just didn't hear Lisa's cry for help when we were on the phone.

Now I had to let Lisa go. Well, I let school go with a whopping 1.7 grade point average and a letter of academic probation. I let the video store go and rented a small loft apartment close to the Parks Mall, where I found new employment. I slowly let most of my friends go out of apathy to engage. I let church go, then I let myself go. Drugs, alcohol, and depression became my new companions—anything that helped me escape the reality of what my life had been thus far. I tried to forget Lisa. I tried to move on.

During this time, I still had Mike Mitchell, one of my friends from that youth group of so long ago, and a few others. I was also making new friends, some that would continue on well into the future and some who fell away as the seasons changed. Aside from those few friends who challenged me to press forward and never let this life be the cause of my demise, I was done. I was back to nothing. No one would guess it from my outward appearance, but I was living a tortured life on the inside.

Lisa would still haunt my dreams, leaving me to wake, frantically searching for her in my conscience world, only to realize that her presence and her love would only be found in my subconscious for a time. I looked forward to sleep, hoping, longing to see my Lisa. I needed to let her go.

Subconscious Me

When I see you, something happens inside me. I disappear and only you exist. No matter what my task at hand is, all my thoughts go to you: "When will I see you again? How will I get to you? How will you look when I see you?"

Sometimes I think that I am talking to someone, then I realize I haven't heard a word. I was thinking of you. When I touch you, even then, when I think I am enjoying you right in front of me, the subconscious me is even more intoxicated by your aroma, your warmth, your piercing blue eyes. I love you, and subconsciously, I love you even more!

Chapter 13

THE BRIDGE

Was this forest that my heart was trapped in destined to be my home? I was growing accustomed to it. My eyes were starting to adjust to the dark, the fetid air unaffectedly mingled with all the other scents emanating from my decaying perception of the state of my life going forward. The creaking of the trees became the lullaby of my restless existence, while the open meadow seemed to be forever out of reach.

As time passed, I started to realize that I was becoming part of that awful forest. I was putting down roots as if I were some sapling tree that should accept its fate, stay put, and grow up here as part of the darkness that surrounded me. I would gaze far off into the heavy thickness of the forest, desperately hoping to catch a glimpse of Lisa, who was perhaps wandering in the same direction as me. I could not see Lisa. I was carrying hopelessness with me as if it were a millstone hanging by a chain around my neck, weighing me down, causing me pain, pulling my head down, preventing me from seeing any light that might be ahead.

While I pictured life as a forest that Lisa and I had walked into together, holding hands before we had been separated, I found a real park in Arlington, Texas, where I would take refuge. It was a beautiful park with a large open field surrounded by a paved trail for walking, jogging, Rollerblading, and such. The field was well kept and litter free with small patches of trees for shade where one might picnic or read poetry. On one side of the field, there was a playground where the sounds of children's laughter floated, like incense, toward heaven. The paved trail broke off at the back of the field and proceeded into a wooded trail, where it made a tee going north and south with a large creek on its west. Each direction of the trail was at least a one-and-a-half-mile walk. The dappled sunlight filtering in through the trees, the gentle breeze bringing the fragrances of pine and honeysuckle, and the rippling waters of the creek playing into the concert of the birds singing above presented a picture of what the forest should be when love is not stifled and all is well. This was the place where I took refuge.

I Miss You

I miss you as the girl I wooed when we were so young.
I miss you as my first and only wife.
I miss the life we could have had together.
I miss the family we should have had together.
I miss all the laughter that would have filled our home—the laughter of you, me, and the children we would have known.
I miss all the time we would have spent playing with our kids.
I miss the unity we would have shared in raising our children.
I miss the hard times we had. They were a blueprint for how I would do everything so very differently than I did before.
I miss the opportunities I have had when failed to act.
I miss how we used to sing in church.
I miss our ministry as youth pastor and wife.
I miss our entire life.
I miss you and me without regrets.
All these things I miss are true, but one thing I will never miss is saying "I love you."

An Excerpt from "A Prayer for My Love"

Years later, I found myself walking down a wooded trail beside a gently flowing creek in Arlington, Texas. It was a beautiful spring afternoon. The air was crisp, and there was a feeling of freshness all around. But I was not happy. This was the place I would come to for solitude. This was the place where I thought I could, at least momentarily, escape the turmoil my life had become. I would think and reflect and ponder my existence. I would call on God in the cool of the garden, and on this day, that is exactly what I did.

I was in my park in Arlington. I had gone for a walk down one of the paved trails. It was much like that night I walked out into the muddy field and screamed at God, only this time, everything was beautiful, and I was not screaming. I was praying. I remember casually glancing from side to side now and then to take in the scenery. On my left, it was a substantially wooded area, which reminded me of my emotional state. The right side of the trail stood in stark contrast, with a sparsely wooded shoulder that dropped off about ten feet down to meet a wide creek whose amiable waters peacefully flowed along as though they were washing away all the despairing thoughts of the day.

I walked along in that edge of a breakdown mode. I was tired of being tired and was tired of being lonely. I hadn't taken any real steps to improve my condition since the night I made the phone call from that little video store, hoping for redemption but receiving an unspecified penance. At this point, I thought I knew that I would never see Lisa again. I thought that she was beyond my grasp forever. Would I remain celibate? Wisdom would suggest that the answer to that question was yes. My answer was "I don't know," but I was out here in the park, on the trail, for a reason. God knew the reason.

I came upon what I have always remembered as an unfinished bridge that would have extended across the creek had it been there in its entirety, probably about fifty feet. The bridge was constructed of wood with handrails attached on either side. They were around three and a half feet high, and the entire bridge was a rusty brown color. It only extended out a short way. You could see the concrete pillars standing out of the water like giants charging a toll for passage across.

Over the years, my mind had taken these images from different places and constructed them in my memory to form this bridge, and it has served to keep the details of what transpired there intact. However, the actual scene was more of a wooden pier that extended from a widened shoulder from the right side of the trail and ended in an observation deck just over the edge of the creek. For this book's purpose, I will call it a bridge. I walked out to the end of the bridge and stood looking over the shimmering waters of the creek, the majestic tree line on the other side, and the distant horizon as the sun hung low in the sky. Tears began to stream down my cheeks as I lifted my eyes up to heaven, up to God.

I thought back to my words: "I will never love again." I began to cry as I implored God, "Please, please, please, dear Heavenly Father. Send me the woman who will love me as much as I love her!" I had realized that my heart did want to love, but I had given the love of my life away. I had nothing left but to ask God for a second chance, to give me the woman whose love I could not throw away.

For a moment that seemed like an eternity, I heard nothing but the light rustling of the leaves on the trees as the wind gently passed through them. I slowly began to hear the soft ripple of the water flowing in the creek beside me. Then I heard God say, "I have sent you what you have asked for." My heart leapt and began to warm. Joy began to rise within my spirit. God heard me and answered.

Chapter 14

Looking for the Promise

So this young lover who had found actual, authentic, legitimate, tangible, bodily, and bona fide love all those years ago in the one he had called "stink bomb," girlfriend, fiancée, and wife would now begin a journey. It had gone from Brad to Brad and Lisa to Lisa and Brad to Mr. and Mrs. Brad Llano. It was "us." Then it was gone. The forest had drawn us in and pulled us apart. It had choked out our dreams and left us lonely and lost. Our future was a vapor that would dissipate when we neared it. The journey for Brad was to be filled with many crossroads, which, to tell about, would fill many volumes. This work is titled *Love Letters to Lisa*, so I will only expound on what is necessary to bring you, the reader, into the proper understanding of my life as it related—and still relates—to Lisa.

I began the process of putting my life back in order. Remember, God had spoken. Now it was up to me to start moving in the right direction. There was now a picayune light stabbing through the massive foliage of the forest I was hacking my way out of. Along the way, I still surveyed, with squinted eyes, my surroundings for a glimpse of Lisa. In the real world, I would see Lisa walking in the distance ahead of me in the mall. I would catch a glimpse of her walking on the sidewalk of some city street in a crowd of people. Every time I tried to catch up to her, the crowd would get thicker, and she would vanish. My mind wasn't playing tricks on me—my heart was.

Over the years, my career path changed many times, and I met all the people groups of the world. My life experiences grew, but where was "the one"? God had said, "I have sent you what you have asked for." I had asked for the one who would love me as much as I loved her.

It was the year 2000; the millennium had arrived. It had been eleven years since the divorce had brought its destruction and desolation. I had recently made the move to San Antonio, Texas, where I worked as an entertainer in a nightclub. I was a comedian, a singer, a dancer, a choreographer, and a disc jockey. I had also held the positions of bouncer, bartender, and even club manager over the last several years. I had moved to San Antonio out of necessity, not desire. My position at a nightclub in Dallas had come to an unexpected end, and I had nowhere to go. My old friend Mike Mitchell was living in San Antonio at this time with his new family, and he extended the invitation for me to bunk at his house until I could get on my feet. I graciously accepted the invitation and their hospitality, packed my clothes, sold most of my belongings for gas money, and made the trip that led to the next milestone in my life.

One month was the approximate duration of my time at the "Casa de Mitchell." I secured employment as a nightclub DJ, moved into a one-bedroom apartment, borrowed a copy of *Moby Dick* for my downtime entertainment, and began the slow trudge out of the forest. Could I do it? Would I make it back to any kind of a normal life? Was there someone out there who was God's answer to my prayer from so long ago?

Two years went by. I worked at the club, bought a few pieces of furniture for my apartment, and visited with the Mitchells as often as possible. I was growing tired of the nightclub life and wanted to move back to North Texas. Then one Friday evening, while I spun seventies and eighties tunes, a new patron came into the club. She stood out from the crowd and did her own thing. She did not seem like the normal clubber, and she caught my eye. As time passed, I learned that she was the same age as me, and she was the single mother of an eleven-year-old boy. She loved classic rock and disco, and she only came out to the club on the weekends that her son was visiting his father. We started becoming friends in the nightclub, and I became her favorite DJ. This woman, like me, had a somewhat sordid past and was reintroducing herself to church. I saw in her a lot of myself, and it seemed like we were on the same path. Could this be who God was sending?

We dated and I met her son. We had dinners, watched movies, and had long conversations about the hardships of life, love, and relationships. Eventually, we were married. It was May 11, 2002, thirteen years after I had divorced Lisa. And now I had a new wife and a new son. I am not going to describe the following nineteen years I spent in that marriage because, as I have said before, this book is *Love Letters to Lisa*. What you do need to know is that over that nineteen-year span of time, I endeavored to be the best husband and father I could possibly be. I would constantly make mental notes on how I had failed in my marriage to Lisa then diligently work to correct those behaviors. I would incessantly work to treat my new wife the way I knew I would treat Lisa if she were present. What I didn't realize then was that I was not working on this new marriage. I was working the old marriage—the marriage with Lisa.

What the Future Holds

What does the future hold?

I hold your face in my hands and feel your tenderness course through my veins as I gaze into your sparkling sapphire eyes.

I hold your head against my chest, and my heart begins to compose a love song with no outro.

What does the future hold?

I hold your hand and am reminded of two young lovers united against all odds. It is the act of security, safety, and surety.

I hold you in my embrace as if to signify that I will never let you go. Emotions can't keep us apart. Opinions can't keep us apart. My embrace is my undying pledge that I will hold your love for eternity.

What does the future hold?

The future holds the mystery that is the rest of our life together. The future holds the culmination of our past and present, that wonderful new beginning! The future holds promise. It holds us! Lisa, I love you.

Chapter 15

Meeting at a Funeral

I am not sure how I was informed. I do not recall who told me, but the news was sad. I had known her from my childhood. She had been there as I grew into a young man. The news of her passing left a void in my life. I had to go to her funeral.

Lisa's mother, Donna, had been in an automobile accident along with her husband, her youngest daughter Stephanie, and one of Stephanie's friends. Donna went home to be with the Lord. I received the news and knew that I must attend that funeral. Yes, I mourned Donna's departure from this life. She had been part of my childhood and was Lisa's mother. She had been my teacher, my mother-in-law, my adversary, and even a help when it hurt her to do so. I would pay my respects. But there was another reason for me to be at that funeral: Lisa would be there.

It was July 17, 2003, and I had been married for just over one year. I explained to my wife about that youth group of my past and my need to be at the funeral for friends as well as family. She understood and said that I should go. I remember calling my mother (who still lived in that little country town of Gainesville) and asking if she would accompany me to the service for Donna. Mother acquiesced to my request. She would go with me, and the two of us would sit quietly in that small church in Gainesville, Texas. Mother was supporting her son (knowing he could not come alone) and mourning the loss of a longtime member of her church family, and I was mourning so much more.

I had to ask Lisa about her recollection of this event because I did not trust my own memory in the matter. Here is the text message of Lisa's recollection:

> *We had her visitation an hour before the funeral, so everyone was just sort of milling around, visiting. I had seen you, Brad, and your mom walking into the church from the parking lot while we were getting out of our car, so I was already looking for you when I got inside. I think I had started talking with some old friends, then you walked up to me and hugged me. I don't remember what we said at that point. We all talked for a minute then I went around to greet some other people. Then a bit later, I saw y'all sitting in the pew, and I came and sat in front of you, and we started talking more. That's when you told me that you had gotten married and that you had a stepson. I said congratulations even though I was sad. We parted. Then I hugged you again when everyone was filing by the family to view her casket. That was the last time I saw you…until Mike's funeral.*

I knew why I was there. Yes, I mourned the death of someone I had known; but more than that, I mourned the death of my first marriage. I saw Lisa there with her new husband and two children, and I was overwhelmed with the emotions that lay siege to my heart that day. I was glad that my Lisa had the things she wanted in this life: a husband, children, a family. I was sorrowful that I had been replaced—that this family was not mine. I was filled with remorse that I had ever let go of her precious hand as we stumbled into the horrible forest of years past. I was angry at everyone who never said "Don't do it, Brad! You must hold on to her and never let go!" I was afraid she would never forgive me, that she would forever hate me.

We hugged, we talked. We were okay, at least on the outside. It was on that day that I realized that Lisa would always be alive in my heart. I would never stop loving her, and why would I? Lisa was my first.

Wanting to Write

I want to write to you, but I see your beautiful joyful face next to the last text you wrote, and I start to stare. My mind begins to wander, and I find myself picturing every expression I can ever remember you making.

I ponder the moments we've had that made us laugh, cry, jump, or just gaze into each other's eyes and bathe in the love we have felt for each other.

I see your face in my mind, your mesmerizing, almost hypnotic, deep blue eyes. Then I feel my heart tremble. I momentarily forget to breathe. My thoughts swirl, and the earth on which I stand ceases to turn on its axis! What just happened? Oh, that's right. I looked at your picture.

I want to write volumes for you and about you. I want to declare my love for you from the highest peaks in the farthest land so that the entire world would know my love for you!

I just realized that I haven't touched a key in several minutes. Why am I not writing? Your face, once again, your gaze… Even though it is only a captured image of you on my phone, it has captured my attention and stirred my heart to quiet adoring reflection. God has given you the ability to hold my heart in your loving grasp.

You have me. I am yours. I love you.

Chapter 16

A PROPHETIC DREAM

Two years later, my wife and I had a daughter. My family was growing. We had a nice house with a back yard that our family dog could run and play in. We also had a front yard where we would sit under a tree sipping Kool-Aid while surveying the activity in our neighborhood. The kids were shooting basketballs on driveway goals and playing Frisbee in the street, and the parents were discussing their trials at work. It was the picture of "normal" American family life, was it not?

The years continued to move past as leaves that had fallen from the trees and been caught in the winds of time, which blew them away as fast as they came. Our children grew, and our careers changed. We were plugged in at the church we attended, we had neighbors and friends, and everything was as it should be. That being said, I was also on meds for anxiety after doing a stint with a psychiatrist for panic attacks and anger issues. Still, this was all part of a "normal" life, right? I was still doing my best to be what I was supposed to be in this family. I was busting my hump, earning my keep, doing my part, raising my kids, and paying attention to my wife. I wasn't slacking!

Here's the thing: I wasn't faking anything. I loved my wife and my family. I had had many wonderful times with this family of mine, and I would do anything to protect them. But what I did not understand at the time was when I would go to sleep in my king-sized bed, next to my wife of many years now, and peacefully fall asleep, I would sometimes dream of Lisa. Lisa and I would have conversations. We would go on walks, we would sit and gaze into each other's eyes, and we would be together as we always should have been. Then I would wake up. Where was I? Who was I with? Was Lisa waiting for me to fall back to sleep so we could resume our life in this other world? Why couldn't I let her go?

I dreamed of Lisa sporadically over the years. She always wore a fur coat like the one she had worn in a senior class photo from the eighties. Lisa's hair was dark and styled as she wore it when we were married. Time stood still in my dreams of Lisa, except for one.

It was 2014. I worked in the survey department of a pipeline construction company. It had been a long day at work, and I was exhausted. When evening came, it was as welcome as the prodigal son, returned home from afar. I remember telling my wife about my day while playing a little Frisbee in the street and laughing with my daughter over a game of *Mario Kart.* Then I was down for the count. It was time for me to go to bed. Sleep fell upon me like an avalanche, ushering in that dream world I knew so well, only this dream was different.

I found myself walking alone in an unknown city, and I came to an open area, much like a large patio. It was nighttime, and I could not tell if it was a clear or cloudy evening. This garden plaza was an outdoor dining patio with concrete flooring, octagonal tables, and benches that fit around them. And at the center of each table was a retractable cloth umbrella that could be raised for shade in the daytime. But at this point, they were closed. The patio was connected to a large two-story building constructed of cream-colored brick, which provided the right-side enclosure for this garden patio if you were looking at it from the street. The left side of the patio had a low barrier, leaving that side fairly open. Straight to the back was what looked like an old New Orleans–style hotel staircase with small balconies at each floor. There was foliage on either side of the staircase, and to the right, between the stairs and the brick wall of the building, was a narrow step down to a landing just beneath the stairs with a wooden gate on the right.

As I peered into the courtyard, I saw Lisa standing by one of the tables. I walked over to her, and we began to converse. There was an eeriness about the setting that I couldn't understand. The lighting was subdued, as if there were a light fog, yet everything was visible. Lisa looked as she always had except that she wore slacks with a black blouse and no fur coat. Our conversation wasn't heated, but it seemed that we were covering material of a serious nature, although the content eludes me now. At one point, Lisa stopped the conversation and informed me that she had business to attend to on the other side of the gate. Then she bid me stay and wait for her.

Lisa walked to the small opening at the back of the patio, down the two steps to the landing. She turned to her right, opened the gate, and went through. I stood in the middle of this eerie, unknown yet familiar concrete garden patio and waited for Lisa's return. After several minutes (which felt like years), I decided to see what was beyond the gate. Where did it lead? I slowly moved to the gate and discovered that there was no lock on it. I pulled the handle and walked through, discovering another smaller patio area. While the first part of the plaza was void of anyone but Lisa and me, this annex had others in it, sitting at the tables, eating and talking, and enjoying the atmosphere. I made a visual inspection of the entire area, looking for the one I had lost. Then, as if she had appeared out of thin air, Lisa was walking toward me, only now she wore a white blouse, and she was smiling as she approached. Lisa embraced me and said, "Finally, you're here!"

Then my peripheral vision began to fade inward. The sky was dissolving downward, and the ground was no longer under my feet. Lisa's smile was the last thing to disappear just before I woke up to the sound of my 5:00 a.m. alarm letting me know that the dream was over, and it was time to get ready for work. That morning, I was still wiping tears from my eyes when I pulled into my parking space at work.

A Love Letter to Brad

My soul has always been connected to you. That's why I have always felt so lost. You were created for me! I have no doubt.

You asked me what it was that made me fall in love with you back then. I gave you a shallow answer, that it was because you were superhot, and I just felt extremely lucky that you wanted to date me! That just makes it sound like I was a giddy schoolgirl infatuated with her older boyfriend, and I guess maybe that's what it was at first. As time went on and I realized how special you made me feel and how you had my back when I felt no one else did, I knew I loved you. I felt so safe with you. You were everything to me!

After we split up, I tried to doubt all the feelings I ever had for you. It was me, by myself, against the world again! I told myself that we couldn't have actually been in love. I believed that maybe what we had was truly just infatuation and that I would move on, and my feelings for you would fade. But my head was just trying to protect my heart.

I moved on, but my feelings never faded. I had to repress those feelings over and over again, and I had to let them live on a different plane than where my actual reality was playing out. They surfaced so many times as dreams and as tearful memories, but I just kept pushing them down, praying to forget. If I ever heard your name or saw your face, every single feeling, emotion, and memory immediately came flooding back. This all proved to me that I had never stopped loving you.

For our paths to now be meeting again after all the life we've lived apart, and for our feelings to have fallen right back into place like we never took a breath, just leaves me in awe. Brad, you are a wonderful man. I love that you are so kind and giving, that you are authentic, that you are funny, that you are an extremely hard worker who doesn't shirk his responsibilities, that you love your daughter so deeply, that you are humble before God and sincerely want His will. I trust your heart. I can truly say that I loved you from the start, that I've never stopped loving you, and that for all the qualities about you that I've just listed, I am actually falling hard for you all over again.

Chapter 17

Two Divorces and a Funeral

The hands of time care not which events are carried along by their steady movement. They do not fret over circumstances or situations. They do not stand still; there is no stagnation in them.

The winds of change are inevitable; they are constant. No barometric reading holds influence with them. They blow where they will with rearranging force.

Once the hourglass has been turned, the sands will make their inexorable, inescapable, unalterable journey to their unpreventable destination.

Change, for better or worse, must and always does happen.

The month of May heralds in change every year: the end of the school year, the end of spring, and in the year 2021, the end of my marriage. I was fifty-four years old—one year away from the "senior discount." May 11 would mark my nineteenth wedding anniversary, and I was totally unaware of what else it would mark. My wife informed me that she had experienced an existential crisis of sorts and that she had no faith in me going forward in our marriage. She expressed to me how she thought that I was a good hardworking man and a wonderful father, but she saw a better future for herself on her own.

While that event was unfolding in my life, another end was coming. My dear friend, Mike Mitchell, was in the ring for the final round with his adversary of many, many years: cancer. I had made a trip to North Texas just weeks before my wife had delivered her revelation to me, for what would be my last in-person visit with Mike.

Mike's situation was not a sudden one, and those of us who knew him were already trying to prepare ourselves for the inevitable. I moved out of my house at the end of May with all my worldly possessions, which, surprisingly, fit into the one bedroom and spare room of a friend's house. This friend put me up, and that bedroom became my home until I could find suitable accommodation for myself and my sixteen-year-old daughter, who was coming with me.

Along with this epoch in my life ending, my dear friend dying, and everything in general being completely overturned in my life, I received a certain clarity. For the last thirty-two years, I had dreamed of Lisa, asked about Lisa, and looked Lisa up on Facebook. But I would not contact Lisa. I had built something into my mind that ate away at me as the mold eats away at the bread left too long. Even though Lisa and I had talked amicably on at least three different occasions over the duration of our separation, I couldn't help but think that she didn't want any communication from me. I thought I was nothing more than a disruption to her mind, heart, and spirit; and if she desired anything from me, she would contact me.

I developed the resolve of Joshua before the wall of Jericho. I had a new philosophy. I would no longer prolong my decisions or passively sit back and let life just happen without my having a say in it. Life was too short for such reckless behavior. I determined that if I felt a genuine need to do something, I would do it. And that I did. I looked Lisa up on Facebook and sent her a friend request. *How appropriate*, I thought. "Will you be my friend?" Lisa responded and we immediately began filling in the information gap that had been our lives. I heard no animosity, no blaming tones, no anger—only that caring, gentle voice of friendship I knew from decades ago. I asked her if she knew of Mike's condition, to which she replied in the affirmative with a saddened resonance that touched my heart. Lisa's reply was by Messenger, but I heard it as I have described it all the same. I ended that conversation by letting Lisa know that I would stay in touch and let her know when Mike's condition changed.

In late June, the spring season had ended, and my friend Mike Mitchell had gone on to be with the Lord. It was a terrible time for those of us he left behind to mourn his passing, but we also rejoiced in the fact that Mike was now in the presence of the Lord. I had the details of Mike's upcoming service early on, being that I would be one of the pallbearers. I let Lisa know all the logistics and added that I would personally love to see her there. Lisa did not know, at this time, that I was going through a divorce. She believed me to still be happily married. I'm quite sure that Lisa heard only an old friend in need, and with all the generosity of her caring heart, she assured me that she would be at the funeral.

The day of Mike's memorial service arrived, not unlike a train pulling into the station to collect precious cargo while, at the same time, making a special delivery. I traveled alone to North Texas. My soon to be ex-wife would not attend with me for fear of the awkwardness of the situation, and my daughter's presence was required at her place of employment. I was the only pallbearer who was not a direct relation of Mr. Mitchell, and while I considered it an immense honor and comfort to be counted as one of their own, I still needed one of my own to comfort me.

As the time neared for the service to begin, people were being ushered into the sanctuary to be seated. Several attendees were still milling about in the foyer, and I stood as a statue made of stone. I waited and watched and wondered if Lisa would arrive soon. Then the front doors to the church opened, and the sun shone in to backlight the woman who had just stepped into the room. With angelic halo and mysterious silhouette, I knew who it was. Lisa was here, and with her came the comfort I so desperately needed. It was like the dream, only I was the one thinking, *Finally, you are here.* Lisa stood among the small crowd, glancing from side to side, searching for someone, anyone she might recognize. I approached, and our eyes met. We shared a smile, which was followed by a hug. In that moment, I could see with such explicit comprehensibility the forest all around us. We had found each other; our paths had diverged. I wasn't cognizant of which path we were on, whether it was acquaintance, renewed friendship, friends from a distance, or just this once. But for the first time since that dreadful day when I stood motionless at the bottom of the courthouse steps thinking, as the attorney drove away, *What have I done?* we were together. I hesitated to release Lisa from my embrace for fear that she would vanish as she had in so many dreams before. I believe that Lisa understood that the hug I gave was more than just a welcoming to the memorial service that was soon to follow.

The service commenced, and the emotion that filled the sanctuary of that little church in DeSoto, Texas, was palpable. The air was saturated with grief mixed with joy. Pain and comfort mingled as loved ones mourned. After the service concluded, the announcement came that there would be a graveside event for all who wished to attend. Here, testimonials were given, and songs were sung. Old friends reunited, discussing the here, now, and what was to come.

1970

The year my love was born, and I didn't even know it yet. I was only three years old. Isn't it interesting how God uses time to impress on us just how important something is?

From unknown to fifty-two years in the future to fully bring a couple together.

After the formalities had come to a close and all condolences were given, I found Lisa. She was waiting just outside the edge of the crowd—waiting to talk with me. We engaged in the usual small talk, of which two strangers might engage, then reassured each other that there were no hard feelings or ill will between us. I extended my gratitude to Lisa for her consolation in my time of grief. Eventually, we had to say goodbye and go our separate ways. It was a bittersweet meeting. I had given no information about my impending divorce, and she had said nothing of having her own marital issues. One thing I did was secure permission to stay in touch. If it was in my power, we would never drift apart again.

We did stay in touch. We were becoming friends, and I was ecstatic. We texted and used Messenger, and we played catch-up. We talked about our families and the paths our lives have gone down over the years. We conversed about our children and the fact that Lisa held the coveted title of Mimi, being the proud grandmother of her daughter's one-year-old son. It was amazing how our conversations had more substance to them than ever before, and the honesty with which we discussed all matters under the sun finally brought me to the hour at which I had to tell Lisa my full situation.

It was, by now, the end of summer and approaching the autumn season. I was trying to come to grips with everything that had happened so suddenly over the summer months. I was attempting to put things in their right place. I needed counsel, and I sought Lisa as my counselor. I would like to share with you a message I sent to Lisa on the last day of August 2021:

> *So here's the deal. Losing Mike has left a large void in my life. I think you, more than anyone else, knows this. Not only were we connected by years and shared experience, but he was also my only link to you. Please don't think this is weird, but Mike managed to never let me completely lose you. I know that you have a wonderful family, and I'm certain that you rival even Nanny in the awesome grandmother department. I praise God for this, but I have to confess that you have never left my heart. That being said, I feel the need to be totally honest with you. Only weeks before Mike's passing, my wife of nineteen years announced that she was divorcing me. She wants a more affluent lifestyle and does not want to continue down the ministry road we embarked on. My heart is broken, and at the age of fifty-four, I feel like I am at square one.*

Lisa listened, counseled, and prayed with me. This was the friend I needed. The next day, I called for the first time. We reminisced about the youth-group days and songs she and I had sung for our church. I sent her a few via text along with a few sermons I had preached recently per my ministerial training. Lisa told me that she would be going on a family vacation to Colorado in the middle of the month, and I gave her my guarantee that I would be praying for her and her family. The next time we texted (after their return from Colorado), Lisa told me that her marriage had been in trouble for years. There had been separations and quarrels, and the state of that marriage had deteriorated to the point that she was pursuing a divorce. I have to be perfectly clear about the fact that neither Lisa's nor my divorce had anything to do with our reunion at the funeral. The timing, however, was extraordinary.

God Created Us

"So God created mankind in His own image, in the image of God He created them; male and female He created them. God blessed them… God saw everything that He had made, and it was very good."

God, with great wisdom and creative knowledge; in the perfection of His plan, created man and woman for each other, and He placed a blessing on that creation. He saw his creation, and it was very good!

God created us, you and me (Brad and Lisa), and He placed His blessing on us. God looked on us, and I believe He said, "They are meant to be very good together." When God designed and formed me, He must have already had your design in mind because we were designed to fulfill God's plan for our lives together.

My love for you has been within me since my youth. Before I even realized what it meant, my love for you was being cultivated.

Like Adam and Eve, we took matters into our own hands and were made to leave the garden. Unlike Adam and Eve, we have been allowed the high honor of tasting the joy of the garden once again.

Lisa, my wish is to work with you in this life, to learn your heart and mind, and to be a comfort, security, and satisfaction for you. You are the desire God has put in my heart. You are the flame that burns so bright before my eyes. You are the soothing breeze that calms my soul.

Your beauty was created for me to behold as the enticement of your affection. Your gentle spirit was created as a safe haven for me in times of despair. Your steadfast devotion has been placed in you as a lighthouse to ever guide me to you when I've lost my way.

God created us for each other, and it is very good. I love you!

Chapter 18

OUT OF THE FOREST

The two young lovers—that newlywed couple, Lisa and Brad—walked into the forest still trying to hold hands. However, somewhere along the way, they lost their grip.

Lisa and Brad had stumbled and tumbled and fallen farther and farther apart in that forlorn and forbidding forest so, so many years ago. And now, much older and much wiser, they could see the light separating the trees. The paths for Lisa and Brad have been hard and agonizing, but those paths were now beginning to rejoin. Their footing was more sure, and the sounds and smells of the forest were tranquil and aromatic. They had passed through the stench of ignorance and confusion. Lisa and Brad could see through the trees, past the underbrush, into the meadow that lay beyond. Lisa and Brad could see each other.

This once young couple, wide-eyed and in love, were now two people in desperate need of rejuvenation, revitalization, and reunion. They had been battered and beaten, tattered, and torn. Lisa and Brad had been scratched by the thorns and thistles of an unrelenting life of separation; the scars ran deep. Now the salve of friendship, the balm of comradery, was performing its soothing work. Lisa and Brad were finally talking to the two people who could truly understand what they were talking about. They were talking to each other.

Step-by-step, they left the eroded trails that had brought them to this convergence. Hand in hand, they pushed the vines apart and pressed through the thicket. Lisa and Brad were there for each other, and they could smell the fresh air blowing across the meadow, bringing with it the tantalizing perfume of newness, of relief. They breathed the bouquet of joy for the first time in a long time. As they stepped out into the open field, the grass moved like the waves of a gentle sea after the tempest had subsided. The sky above, a vast canvass with its azure hues, held the flocculent white clouds in place, providing shade lest the brilliant sun, with its magnificent rays, shone too bright for eyes that, for so long, had been accustomed to the dark. Everything around Lisa and Brad now looked new, felt new, and sounded new.

Lisa and Brad stood in that field, freed from the forest. They stared into each other's eyes and began to know peace. This end of the forest that had beset them on all sides was the beginning of something new.

From the Meadow through the Forest

Two young lovers hold hands as they walk through a meadow on a cool spring afternoon. The air is crisp as a breeze gently blows across the meadow grass, which looks like gentle rolling waves on an open sea. The sky is an exhilarating blue, spreading across the young lovers as if to suggest, the world is theirs and the possibilities of their life together are limitless. The two young lovers hold hands.

As they walk along, the young woman gazes at the young man beside her. She knows that the truest love has entered her life. She will never give up true love! The young man kisses the young woman. This kiss is one of undying passion and devotion. The young man knows there could not, would not, ever be a kiss from another that would rival the spark, the igniting explosive experience that signified the powerful love of this young couple. The two young lovers hold hands with interlocking fingers.

The light spring breeze starts to increase as soft white clouds begin to populate the once clear blue sky. The clouds provide shade while the lovers cross the meadow, approaching a tree line that is the entrance into the unknown. The couple enters the forest fully believing they will find the open meadow on the other side. They clutch each other's hands.

As the two walk hand in hand through the forest, the sunlight struggles to penetrate the foliage above. The man and woman continue to talk as their grips loosen. The ground is stony with short stubbly grass.

The forest wildlife has made strange trails that connect and cross over one another, causing confusion and apprehension when trying to decide a correct path to follow through the forest. The man and woman find themselves walking distant from each other as they try to navigate the darkness of the forest; they have strayed on to separate paths.

As they both stumble, stagger, and succumb to the obstacles of this densely wooded forest, they call to each other. Each one is just in sight but always out of reach!

When all the memories have nearly faded away and true love's kiss seems but a fantasy, when the darkest cloud seems to suffocate the rays of the sun that once shone so brightly upon two young lovers, when all seems lost, the meadow appears. The forest has ended.

The older man has been beaten down but not out. The mature woman has the scars of life upon her soul. She stands in the open meadow and looks to the left. He stands in the open meadow and looks to the right. Their eyes meet; their embrace is rejoined. She never let go of true love, and he kisses her, not with a fantasy kiss but with that passionate devotional kiss that only she could return. They have gone from the meadow through the forest. The two old lovers hold hands.

Chapter 19

Reconciliation

Lisa left Tyler, Texas, and traveled across the Red River into Oklahoma, where she sojourned at her sister and brother-in-law's home. The conversations between us had turned into an almost daily routine of discussions on theology and family, our relationship and our new friendship, and the issues that were on our hearts: our children. We talked about Mike Mitchell's passing and how I was handling it, and we prayed together. If this was all that would ever become of Lisa and me, I could have lived happily ever after. She was back in my life, and I was in hers. We had become, once again, an integral part of each other's lives, and this was what I had needed for so many seasons past in my life.

Lisa texted: "Can I call you? There is something I want to ask you about." I replied: "I will have some time before I have to be at work tomorrow." Then I gave her a time to call. I wanted to be sure that I had all the time I needed to hear whatever Lisa had to say or ask, so the following day, I made sure to be at work in plenty of time to receive Lisa's call and talk, uninterrupted, for as long as she needed. I was in the employee parking lot, in the farthest space from the front I could find. I waited in my vehicle with the windows rolled halfway down and my seat slightly reclined. It was a beautiful autumn afternoon. The sun was providing warmth, and the sparse cloud cover provided the shade. I was comfortable, and I had over an hour to talk before I needed to clock in for the half-shift I had picked up for that day.

My cell phone rang, and I answered. Lisa said hello. Let the conversation begin. We began with all the general opening pleasantries, and nothing in our conversation seemed very pressing. Then Lisa was momentarily silent. I remained silent. The silence was deafening, and this seemed familiar somehow. Wait a minute. A long-distance phone call, me on one end and Lisa on the other, "something I want to ask you about," and a moment of silence? I had been here before. The words were still rolling off Lisa's tongue when my entire life actually flashed before my eyes. This wasn't a near-death experience that I was having. It was a new life experience! I viewed every moment leading up to my beginning with Lisa, every memory we had ever shared, every mistake, every misfortune, every laugh, every cry, every intimate moment between us as if I was seeing it on the big screen from some supernatural film projector. I was translated through the forest and delivered to the other side.

What was Lisa's query? you ask. She said, "Do you remember what you said when you called me from Arlington?"

I answered yes. Was this really happening? Could this be possible?

Lisa's next question was "Did you mean it?"

I was transported to another plane, one which was neither past, present, nor future. All I knew was that the phone call I had made from a borrowed manager's office in a video store in Arlington, Texas, back in 1992 had come full circle. And now I was being asked if I wanted reconciliation with my first wife, Lisa! Yes, yes, absolutely. The answer was yes!

Lisa and I were laughing and crying at the same time. Everything had just fallen into place like an avalanche that must come to a stop at the bottom of the mountain. What was happening was miraculous, marvelous, and magical. It was supernatural and heaven-sent. I was taking hold of that moment with everything that I was. I would not let it slip through my fingers. These two old "young lovers" stood in that open meadow at the end of the forest and held hands tightly.

The road ahead would certainly present challenges, and we both knew this. We were not living in that fantasy world we started out in. We were serious. It had taken thirty-two years for God to prepare us for what we needed to be for each other. We had the tools to rebuild our relationship, for the one thing we never lost was our foundation. As I recall, from that day forward, we talked every day. And when I say we talked, I mean for hours at a time. All my days had a specific purpose now—to finish work, get back to my bedroom house, and call Lisa.

We decided to meet in October, so I flew to Oklahoma, where I was met at the airport by the coolest girl I had ever seen. She stood at the curb, just outside the arrivals portal. She was leaning on her SUV, her hair blowing in the wind, her shades pulled down, and I went to her and wrapped my arms around her. Being with Lisa was home to me. We continued to talk by phone and text every day. We decided on meeting in person once a month, and nothing could stop us. I would ride hundreds of miles on my motorcycle in bitter cold and rain, with the winds pressing against me all the way, in order to see my Lisa, and she would drive hundreds of miles to meet me halfway. We were falling in love all over again.

In March of 2022, Lisa moved to San Antonio, Texas. Reconciliation, reunion, and restoration—these were our goals. The days of phone calls and texts were far from over, but now we could see each other on a daily basis. We could sit face-to-face and talk over coffee. We could meet for an afternoon lunch or sit on the sofa in the evening at her apartment or mine and cuddle while we watched a movie. This was fresh, new, and a necessary part of the relationship we were rebuilding.

In May of that same year, we rededicated ourselves to each other and renewed our commitment with the buying of rings, two bands of white gold—one beset with diamonds denoting beauty and elegance, the other less resplendent and with no intent to call attention to itself other than to say, "I support and protect the one who is my love."

We have begun the process of learning what blended families are as we meet and interact with each other's children when we make holiday plans and attend grandson birthday parties. We have had many conversations dealing with our past (Lisa's past, my past) and what the future should look like. Thirty-two years of understanding does not come easily, but it does come with great reward. We have been so much more than willing to put in the work required to see the restoration that God has been and currently is bringing into our lives.

Patience

> *pa-tience*
> *Noun:*
> 1. *The capacity to accept or tolerate delay, trouble, or suffering without getting angry or upset.*
> *This word does not suffice.*
> *"If I speak in the tongues of men and of angels, but do not have love, I have become a noisy gong or a clanging cymbal" (1 Corinthians 13:1 NIV).*
> *So I am not a patient man. I am a man in love, and patience is only one element in the equation of love that I may exhibit showing my love to be true.*
> *"Love is patient, love is kind. It does not envy, it does not boast, it is not proud. It does not dishonor others, it is not self-seeking, it is not easily angered, it keeps no record of wrongs. Love does not delight in evil but rejoices with the truth. It always protects, always trusts, always hopes, always perseveres. Love never fails" (1 Corinthians 13:4–8 NIV).*

Within me, there is a great love for you. I try to live God's Word in all aspects of my life, and I often fail miserably. I think, hope, and believe that my love for you has not failed.

You are the object of my affection! I love you, baby.

How it started   How it's going

Chapter 20

Putting It All Together

I said earlier in this book that I would come back to a few things. Allow me to now clarify those earlier things.

There is much work to be done if two people are to successfully cultivate a lifelong partnership of trust, adoration, affection, consideration, and commitment. This is called covenant. Love's true meaning encapsulates all things necessary to form, bind, and honor a lasting covenant. Unfortunately, we don't always understand the true and full meaning of love.

In the love letter I incorporated in the last chapter (Patience), there is a quote from 1 Corinthians 13:4–8, and it clearly defines love. Many have read these verses from 1 Corinthians but haven't really inspected what it is saying. Let me lay open what this passage means to me.

"Love is patient." In this simple phrase, I see that time is irrelevant when I consider the duration of my true love. There is no point at which I become weary of loving my unfeigned intended. The clock doesn't run out on love.

"Love is kind." I believe this means that I should constantly be looking for ways to fulfill a measure of joy in the one I love. Her happiness brings me happiness, and when she is content, it pleases me.

"It does not envy, it does not boast." When the love of my life succeeds in any endeavor, it gives me a certain exuberance. I encourage and give praise. I do not boast. My mission is to put Lisa first. I exist in order to protect, provide, and promote Lisa, not myself.

"It is not proud." This is actually defined by the following verse: "It does not dishonor, it is not self-seeking, it is not easily angered, it keeps no record of wrongs." My job is not to be the keeper of faults and imperfections. When given the choice (and it is always a choice) between letting anger have its way and going back to "love is patient," choose patience. Anger is a destroyer and has no business in a true loving relationship.

"It always protects, always trusts, always hopes, always perseveres." I defer you to the wedding vows. "To love, honor, and cherish" could easily be translated as "to always protect the heart, the spirit, and the body," and trust that you don't always know everything. A partner contributes. Always hope for the light in the darkness, the sun behind the clouds, and the meadow beyond the forest. Persevere when it is difficult to hope.

Next is the matter of the *prophetic dream* (December 30, 2022). Lisa and I had made a journey up to Tyler, Texas, for overnight so we could have dinner together and relax after the long drive. The next day, we would have brunch with her daughter and son-in law, give Ollie his Christmas presents, then take him for a quick trip to the park before we had to drive back to San Antonio.

That first evening, Lisa wanted to show me downtown Tyler. I had never been to the downtown area of Tyler before and thought it would be fun to stroll around the town square after having a little dinner at one of the local eateries. The square was still decorated with all the trappings of Christmas, presenting a beautiful and festive atmosphere. We took selfies, and we walked hand in hand down the sidewalk, past the small businesses that lined the main street. As we crossed at one of the signal lights and began to walk up the next block, I looked ahead and to my left in astonishment. How could this be? At first, I thought it was déjà vu. But no, this was more than that!

Before me stood a large cream-colored two-story brick building, which housed a coffee shop / bakery. Adjacent to the building, right before my eyes, was an open patio courtyard with concrete flooring, a low brick wall on the left side, and another two-story building forming the back wall. This back building was designed to look like an old New Orleans–style hotel with an outside staircase that had small balconies at each landing. At the ground level, there was foliage on either side of the staircase and a small sunken space underneath the stairs with a wooden gate on the right side. There were several octagonal tables with benches sitting around them. Each table had an umbrella that fit through the center of the table. This was a real place, and I had been here before in a dream!

I thought—as I was frantically telling Lisa about the dream I had back in 2014—that she might think I was a little crazy. I told her, while we stood in the middle of the courtyard, about the sunken area with the gate. I then ran to the back of the courtyard, and the sunken area was there along with the gate. I kept talking in rushed and frenzied tones about the coloring of the walls, the tables, the somewhat foggy yet clear setting of the evening—everything! Then, without seeing it, I described what lay beyond the gate behind the building in order to offer irrefutable proof that this was no coincidence. Then I took Lisa inside and asked the server at the register what was beyond the gate behind the building? The server described an annex that had recently been added, which matched my description to a tee.

I believe that the dream I had in 2014 was an assurance of things to come. In the dream, I stood talking with Lisa, who wore slacks with a black blouse. We were not in an argument, but the vein in which we were talking was serious and not necessarily jovial. Lisa left at one point, bidding me wait while she took care of some business. Lisa left through the gate at the back. After some time and her failure to return, I went looking for her. I went through the gate into the next dining area, where Lisa, now in a white blouse, came to me smiling and saying, "Finally, you're here!"

I believe the serious conversation with Lisa in dark colors was representative of the time we were apart from each other but could never fully let go. When I went through the gate, it was a different time, and Lisa came to me in light-colored clothing with a smile and anticipation. This represented our reconciliation, and now we were standing in real time, realizing the fullness of the event. It was amazing!

One more thing before I release you from my story, leaving you to your own. That prayer at "The Bridge" was a prayer for the one who would love me as much as I loved her. God gave me an answer that day. He said, "I have sent you what you have asked for." Back then, I thought it meant that God had sent her in reply to my prayer and that I should be on the lookout for her.

From "A Prayer for My Love"

Years later, after the roller coaster of life had left me on the brink of doubt, you walked through the doors of a small church in DeSoto, Texas. The backdrop was the funeral service for a dear friend, a mutual friend; but in the foreground of my mind, heart, and soul was you!

We embraced, and I held you tight, shivering, quivering, and fearing that if I let go, you wouldn't really be there. Then I looked at your face, the most beautiful face. I gazed into your eyes, the most loving eyes. I smelled your fragrance, and I was smitten. All these emotions had to be kept secret for a time. Eventually, in time, love revealed itself. The delight of my heart, the love of my life, became, once again, the delight of my heart and love of my life.

What happened next is the amazing part. I remembered what God had said that day in response to my prayer for love: "I have sent you what you have asked for." It was ALWAYS YOU! Love has never been sweeter, joy has never been fuller, and my happiness has never been more complete. God sent me you, and I can truly feel your love as strong and right for me as mine is for you. We are the best example I can think of for the term "meant to be"!

I have always loved and always will love you, my beautiful, wonderful, and amazing Lisa.

What God was actually saying was I HAVE sent you what you have asked for (already). God had sent me Lisa. Lisa was always the one! Lisa will always be the one, and our story continues.

The Wall

There are six steps to building a stone wall. This is not the only kind of wall there is to build, but let me speak to this for a moment.

The skill level involved is "hard." Stone is heavy, difficult to move, and it often pinches fingers. The cost is "much," roughly $800 every ten feet. The time it takes is "as long as it takes." (How high will the wall be?)

First, you must prepare the footing. This involves digging a trench where the wall will be set: the foundation. Next is laying the base course. This is done by setting the first stone then placing the next one next to it and so on until the first course is laid. Repeat this on the opposite side, and top it with mortar in order to solidify the base course. After this, you must build up the wall. At this stage, you simply lay stone after stone on top of one another, continually filling in with mortar, creating a sturdy wall that will last a lifetime or longer.

The last three steps are to "mark" the stones to cut, "cut" the stones (giving the wall its shape), and "tool" the joints, which is the finishing act.

My dearest Lisa, your life has taught you how to build a wall. Although you have experienced joy at times, peace on occasion, and love not nearly enough, you have lifted the heavy stones that have pinched your fingers and bruised your soul. You have paid the high price of anguish and depression for the materials in your wall. It has been over forty years in the making.

The footing was prepared, which involved digging a trench, the scarring of such an innocent, pure, and loving heart. At such an early age, life began teaching you how to build a wall.

The base course was laid, and the wall began to be built. Stone after stone, one after another, what was once the most beautiful, caring, giving, and loving spirit was being walled up and sealed away.

Lisa, as I ponder God's plan for me concerning you, one thing is perfectly clear. I am to dismantle the wall.

There are actually two ways to bring a wall down. One way is to hammer it apart—destroy it. The other is to gently, with care and consideration, clear away the mortar and remove each stone one by one.

I am here to help you take each stone down one by one. My love for you is the tool required to clear away the mortar holding your wall together. My hope for us and genuine desire to nurture healing in your heart will be the tools needed to remove each one of life's stones from the wall that encompasses you. My longing for an uninterrupted, full, and joy-filled life with you, my true love, will be the cleaning agent that brings restoration for our joined hearts.

God alone can and will restore our souls, our spirits, and His plan for us.

I love you with all that I am.

The Letters

A Love Letter to You

When you walked into the sanctuary, I was unable to breathe. I could barely speak the words I so longed to speak. You said "I do," and my heart leaped within my chest. When our bodies touched, I truly felt we were one. Our life together was interrupted and so prematurely put on hold. The pureness of our love was soiled by the corruption of this would. I died a thousand deaths at the thought of the chasm that lay between us. You never left my heart. I could not—would not—put you away. Now you speak my name and tell me that I have always been your true love. My heart, once again, leaps in my chest, and words vanish from my vocabulary. I am rendered mute, for I cannot find words eloquent enough to express my undying love for you. There are no words strong enough to convey my devotion to you. Let me then keep it simple. I love you, Lisa. I am in love with you. I have always been in love with you, and I know that I always will love you.

On My Mind

So I'm up. I've had my coffee. I made it to work safely. I'm clocked in and thinking about you. You are on my mind when I wake up. You are on my mind while I eat my breakfast. When I say my morning prayers, you are with me there too. When I go to work, I bring you with me. I count the minutes until I can call you, then I don't want to hang up. I think about and wonder what you are doing throughout the day, and I can't wait to call you in the evening to talk about us. I love you with all that I am. I believe that God created me for you. Good morning, Lisa.

Observations at Breakfast

At breakfast, I decided to observe couples that would come in. It was early, so there weren't many, but I noticed that when they came in, they would immediately pick up separate menus and begin searching for the sustenance of their choice. When they received their food, they would start arranging their plates and condiments. There were few endearing glances, and they didn't hold hands. There was not a great deal of conversation. You might surmise that they were a couple that had been together for a long time.

I thought about us. I steal every second to look into your beautiful eyes before you begin to blush. As we walk together and the natural rhythm of our gait brings our hands together, I hold yours in mine as if to suggest that I will never let you go. We could share a menu, and when you ask, "What do you want?" I say "you." We are not a new couple. Though we have been apart for thirty-two years, our love and our relationship is still as fresh as the morning dew. I love you, my beautiful Lisa.

Love Language

Learning a love language isn't the easiest thing to do, but it is probably one of the most rewarding. Saying the words "I love you" is only the beginning of the journey down that difficult road that leads to a beautiful destination. Along the way, we learn when to listen and when to speak. We are careful to try to understand those little nuances in each other's voice that indicate when we are happy, sad, apprehensive, scared, upset, pleased, comfortable, or just plain gushing with love for each other. We discover how to be patient and kind, especially when we want to be defensive and defend our points. We strive to find out what it is that soothes a frustrated tone or brings out a laugh in the midst of turmoil. We love with our eyes. We love with our thoughts. We love with our words and with the work we are willing to put in to help each other grow. We promote peace, and we long to embrace. We are romance's biggest advocate, and we find ways to never let an argument go unresolved. Lisa, I love you! Now I travel down that difficult road to my "beautiful" destination.

I Just Had a Thought

You know how couples say "you're stuck with me" or "I'm sticking with you," and then things happen, and the glue doesn't hold? I think way back in the eighties, God used a heavenly adhesive on us. And when Brother Jackson said, "What God has joined together (or stuck together), let no man tear asunder," I think God included us in that "no man" (or woman) part. We have been stuck together so well that even we couldn't unstick us. Whew! Our God is an awesome God!

Sitting Here Thinking

I'm sitting here thinking, *Can I love you any more than I do right now?* Hold on. Ahhhhh! There! Now I love you even more.

Random Thought

This may sound a little random, but as I was waiting for a plane to arrive at work today, I began to think of our love. You and I tend to express our feelings for each other, the way we care about each other and want to share in each other's troubles, joys, failures, and triumphs. Each of us wants to meet the other's needs and offer encouragement in the face of adversity. We say, "I love you. I have always loved you and always will love you, no matter what."

So here is what I want to tell you. I love your feet because they carry you to me. I love your arms because they embrace me. I love your hands because they so tenderly and lovingly caress me. I love your mouth because it speaks to me what your heart feels. I love your eyes because like cool clear pools of blue water, they entice and soothe me. You are my love, and I love all of you.

1970

The year my love was born, and I didn't even know it yet. I was only three years old. Isn't it interesting how God uses time to impress on us just how important something is? From unknown to fifty-two years in the future to fully bring a couple together.

Thinking of You

I think of you as I start my day. As I prepare myself for the day's work, my thoughts drift back to an image of your beautiful face, which has been forever imprinted on my mind. As I complete the mundane activities of the morning, I imagine us playfully calling to each other from room to room. This makes me smile, and it brings a warmth to my heart. Throughout the day, committing my thoughts to the tasks at hand becomes increasingly difficult because I wonder where you are and how you are feeling. I wonder if you are thinking of me. I wonder if you are happy or sad, working or playing, or maybe just waiting for me to send you a love note? When my workday finally comes to an end, I think of us sitting on a sofa together and holding each other as we relax and unwind. I think of calling you, and I do. Then we talk until the next day begins. We laugh, we cry, we talk sexy, and we finally say goodbye. When I think that I will stop thinking and go to sleep, you come to me in my dreams. I think I love you. I know that I love you, and I am thinking of you right now.

Dreams

You have been a lifetime of dreams for me. We would be together, all would be forgiven. We would make love and plan our future together while we held each other in the afterglow of the preceding ecstasy. Then I would wake up, and all was lost, and the worst part was that I had to go through that alone. Who could I share it with? I have lived a life of being devastated over and over until now. Now it all makes sense, and don't anyone dare pinch me because if I'm not awake and this is only a dream, I will gladly stay asleep forever! I love you so, so, so very much, and I look forward to every minute I can have with you until death do us part (except I don't believe we ever will really part).

A Short Note

We need heavy conversations now and then, but I prefer the fun giggling talks.

Waking Up Thinking of You

I always wake up thinking of you, and that makes me very happy. I will have a good day because I will be thinking of you throughout it. I also love our talks. They continue to reveal how much we are meant for each other. You do help me every day. I only regret that we have missed so many days until now. They say "until death do us part." I LOVE YOU WITH NO UNTILS ATTACHED! To love, honor, and cherish…for richer or poorer, in sickness and in health, through thick and thin for all time. I make this vow to you!

Wanting to Write

I want to write to you, but I see your beautiful joyful face next to the last text you wrote, and I start to stare. My mind begins to wander, and I find myself picturing every expression I can ever remember you making.

I ponder the moments we've had that made us laugh, cry, jump, or just gaze into each other's eyes and bathe in the love we have felt for each other.

I see your face in my mind, your mesmerizing, almost hypnotic, deep blue eyes. Then I feel my heart tremble. I momentarily forget to breathe. My thoughts swirl, and the earth on which I stand ceases to turn on its axis! What just happened? Oh, that's right. I looked at your picture.

I want to write volumes for you and about you. I want to declare my love for you from the highest peaks in the farthest land so that the entire world would know my love for you!

I just realized that I haven't touched a key in several minutes. Why am I not writing? Your face, once again, your gaze... Even though it is only a captured image of you on my phone, it has captured my attention and stirred my heart to quiet adoring reflection. God has given you the ability to hold my heart in your loving grasp.

You have me. I am yours. I love you.

With Solomon's Help

I have been feeling particularly sexual about you today, so I decided to go to God's Word on the subject. I was reading through Song of Songs when I came to the following quote: "You are all together beautiful, my darling; there is no flaw in you... You have stolen my heart, my sister, my bride; you have stolen my heart with one glance of your eyes; with one jewel of your necklace. How delightful is your love my sister, my bride! How much more pleasing is your love than wine, and the fragrance of your perfume than any spice! Your lips drop sweetness as the honeycomb, my bride; milk and honey are under your tongue (Song of Songs 4:7–10 LSV)." There is so much to the relationship we have. There are so many levels: attraction, affection, affirmation, sexuality, sensuality, submission (to God's will and to each other), friendship, partnership, and agreement. Once again, I end with "I love you!"

Without

Dear Lisa, my beautiful companion in so many ways, I enjoy your beauty with an unknown depth. If I were without my vision, I would drink in your scent—an intoxicating aroma that arouses my desire. I would find my way to your warm embrace, knowing you, set apart from all others. I would taste your sweet kisses—kisses that are more satisfying than any nectar this earth produces. I would trace every line of your beautiful face and every contour of your enticing body pressed against mine.

If I were without touch, I would be lost in the rapturous vision of your beauty. I would stare at your crystal-blue eyes and be held captive by your hypnotic gaze. I would look deeply into those lovely refreshing pools of tender affection where your soul is laid bare before me, and with my own eyes, I would declare my never-ending, undying, unwavering love and devotion for you.

If I were without you, all would be lost. Life would be an act. I would find no more human joy. I would have God and eternity to sustain me, but I would not be living the life God created me for. It would be a broken half-life, only to be lived out until death set me free. I will not dwell on such a thought because I am not without. I will love, relish, and pour out my affection on you with all my senses and all that I am, and I will not be broken. I love you!

A Prayer

Heavenly Father, I come to You in the precious name of Your Son, Jesus, the Word, the sacrifice, the one who took the punishment and made the atonement for the sin of all mankind—for me. I worship the name of Jesus and give You praise. I thank You for being the God who listens to His creation's petitions. I thank You for being my Heavenly Father.

This morning, I come to you with my petition. Yesterday afternoon, as I was cleaning Your house (minding the temple), I was frightened by Lisa's words: "I don't want you to worry, but I'm calling to let you know that earlier, I started experiencing chest pains. I went to an urgent care facility, and they want to send me to the hospital by ambulance." Lord, I pleaded with You yesterday to not take Lisa from me so soon, but I also realize that we don't know the number of our days. We are not assured anything more than the last breath we just took.

I pray that You bless and anoint every moment of the life You have brought Lisa and me back to. I pray that You give her health in her body and healing in her spirit. I pray that You mend her heart—her precious heart that has been so badly cared for.

Heavenly Father, I pray for the ability to love Lisa with a love as full as the love You have for me. Help me to show her, in my every expression, the love and passion You have given me for her, the one you created to be my companion.

Heavenly Father, I pray that You help us to cherish every instant, every moment of every day, that You allow us in this second chance to bring our sacrifice of praise, to worship You through the illustration of our love, commitment, and devotion for each other. Heavenly Father, I love You. I praise You, and I thank You for all good things. I thank You for my beautiful Lisa.

Traveling

Today, you began a road trip with your daughter from Oklahoma to points in Northeast and South Texas. You are en route to visit family and friends, to celebrate your grandson's second birthday, to take care of the business that follows a divorce, and then (what I consider the best part) to see me.

I imagine that as you began driving south, you might have experienced a small amount of anxiety due to the impending winter storm that held the threat of interfering with your travel—your travel toward me. There must have been some giddy joy as you started the engine of your rental car and pulled out of the driveway. You were coming to me. There was anticipation in the air—the anticipation of lovers traveling toward a rendezvous where they embrace and kiss and declare their love for each other. We prayed for God's blessing and protection then began the countdown to our reunion.

A long time ago, in a small town in North Texas, you and I started a journey together. We began traveling the road of us. We were full of the anticipation of building our home together. We were looking forward to a union of lovers—to becoming one flesh, one spirit, one heart. We were traveling at full speed. We were unstoppable!

We experienced that giddy joy that young lovers know when they start the car and pull out of their parents' drive and into the driveway of their new life together. However, that impending winter storm hit. It tried to blow us off our road: the road God had placed us on. The cold gusting winds of doubt, fear, and confusion separated us in our travel on that wonderful journey we had begun. We got lost in the darkness of that storm and strained to see the road that would lead us back to each other. Then, all of a sudden, we were back together. We have been so blessed, and I am nothing less than amazed at our story. That full-throttle, unstoppable love has not been stopped. We may have each taken a detour, but our separate roads were always meant to be rejoined. I must proclaim my undying love for my fiancée and partner in life, Lisa.

The Heart Attack

One day, when I was younger, I was walking in a mall. I was happy enough, and it was a pleasant outing. As I walked, I began to have trouble catching a full breath. I started to feel lightheaded, and my left arm began to ache. I wasn't sure why I was feeling this way; I hadn't been ill recently. Then I felt a sharp pain proceeding from my chest outward.

I sat down at the edge of a water fountain and tried to regain my composure. There were people walking past me, having conversations and joyfully shopping. The fountain that I was sitting by was flowing with life and the sound of soothing happiness. I was watching these people bustle and scurry through the mall while I listened to the peaceful murmuring of the fountain beside me as it dawned on me that I was having a heart attack. How could this be? I was only in my thirties. I was healthy, energetic, and fit. I was incredulous! Still, it was happening. Slowly and with difficulty, I went to my car and made it back home. I called work and told them I would not be in that evening. I lay down on my bed and stayed there, not knowing if this would get better or worse. Finally, sleep came. The next day, I went to my doctor, who confirmed my fear. My heart was broken.

The heart's purpose is to sustain life. It does this by beating steadily and rhythmically in order to pump blood throughout the body, transporting what the body needs to stay alive. The heart's function is to love.

We talk about matters of the heart and the affairs of the heart. We say that we give our hearts in love. The emotions of the soul are felt in the heart. When two people fall in love, their hearts begin to sync. They begin to find a shared rhythm in order to beat as one. When this happens and the two hearts are working properly together, synchronous—rhythmically, adoringly, and strongly encouraging, caring for, and supporting each other—then the two hearts that beat as one sustain love. What happens when love has a heart attack, when the two hearts get out of sync? Love suffers. Confusion and pain invade the beautiful flowing meadow of love, turning it into a battlefield. Misunderstanding and doubt war against the two hearts that had become one.

When the dust settles, two hearts are broken and scarred. Love has had a heart attack!

Remember my heart attack at the mall? "What happened after that?" you may ask. Two things happened:

1. God gave me an immediate healing. I had had an irregular heartbeat that had led to a minor coronary. God gave me a regular heartbeat.
2. God gave me a healing over time. Slowly, my heart got stronger and stronger. I have never had another heart attack.

Lisa, our hearts fell in sync a long time ago. They developed a steady, rhythmic beat that became one heart. I believe that our love was and is one of the strongest and most enduring loves known. It has been put into the fire, dragged through the desert, hurled off a cliff, and cast into the depths of the sea. Our hearts have been broken but not destroyed. Life still pumps through the body of our love. These two hearts that God created for us have gone through an immediate and miraculous healing. God reunited us! Our hearts are also going through a healing over time. The only way this makes sense to me is that we will become stronger and stronger over time, and we will never have another heart attack again.

My love for you is patient. I will give you every day that God allows me to live so that your heart may be fully healed. I love you during the times of delight and prosperity, and I love you when the storms rage around us. I love you more than myself. We have survived the heart attack.

I love you.

Dating

Giddy, nervous, excited, anticipatory, hopeful—the emotions of new love. These were the emotions that were welling up inside me as I prepared for our first date. You were so beautiful and inviting, like the first day of spring. Your scent was so alluring, exhilarating… almost inebriating. You had most certainly captured my heart before I even realized it. You possessed a magnetism that drew me to you; it almost seemed primal. We were both so young and eager to really know each other. Though we were young, the time had come to embark on that wonderful time-honored tradition of finding your mate, the one you would spend the rest of your life with…dating.

My dearest Lisa, the one I call Beautiful, it seems an eternity since that first date and all the subsequent dates thereafter. You have remained as fresh in my memories and in my heart as that first electrifying moment in time when I knew I was going to ask you the biggest, most important question of my life: "Will you be my date?" This was the question that opened up a world of romance, passion, and completeness with my true soulmate.

Yes, there have been storms in our life. Yes, there have been obstacles on our path. We even believed, at one point, except for a dream world, our life together was over. It is so thrilling today to not start over but begin again as a new, fresh, rousing couple that can enjoy again the stirring of our hearts as we learn how to truly help, please, and love each other. We are becoming one. We are dating.

A Prayer for My Love

Lisa, I want to share with you a conversation I had one day with God. This is not a historical account or a letter about details. It is a letter about emotions.

I had heard the words "That is it, it's done," but I couldn't believe that, just like that, our marriage had ended. I stood on the sidewalk in front of the Cooke County Courthouse in a fog. In my mind, I wanted to run back into the courthouse and beg the judge to throw away the divorce papers he had just, moments before, so nonchalantly signed into the law that would hang so heavily around my neck for so many years to come.

I didn't run back into the courthouse. I slowly walked away in tears. What had I done?

I told myself that I would never be married again—that I would never love again. My heart was more than broken; it was mortally wounded.

Years later, I found myself walking down a wooded trail beside a gently flowing creek in Arlington, Texas. It was a beautiful spring afternoon. The air was crisp, and there was a feeling of freshness all around. But I was not happy. This was the place I would come to for solitude. This was the place where I thought I could, at least momentarily, escape the turmoil my life had become. I would think and reflect and ponder my existence. I would call on God in the cool of the garden, and on this day, that is exactly what I did.

I thought back to my words: "I will never love again." I began to cry as I implored God, "Please, please, please, dear Heavenly Father, send me the woman who will love me as much as I love her!" I had realized that my heart did want to love, but I had given the love of my life away. I had nothing left but to ask God for a second chance, to give me the woman whose love I could not throw away.

For a moment that seemed like an eternity, I heard nothing but the light rustling of the leaves on the trees as the wind gently passed through them. I slowly began to hear the soft ripple of the water flowing in the creek beside me. Then I heard God say, "I have sent you what you have asked for." My heart leapt and began to warm. Joy began to rise within my spirit. God heard me and answered.

Years later, after the roller coaster of life had left me on the brink of doubt, you walked through the doors of a small church in DeSoto, Texas. The backdrop was the funeral service for a dear friend, a mutual friend; but in the foreground of my mind, heart, and soul was you!

We embraced, and I held you tight, shivering, quivering, and fearing that if I let go, you wouldn't really be there. Then I looked at your face, the most beautiful face. I gazed into your eyes, the most loving eyes. I smelled your fragrance, and I was smitten. All these emotions had to be kept secret for a time. Eventually, in time, love revealed itself. The delight of my heart, the love of my life, became, once again, the delight of my heart and love of my life.

What happened next is the amazing part. I remembered what God had said that day in response to my prayer for love: "I have sent you what you have asked for." It was ALWAYS YOU! Love has never been sweeter, joy has never been fuller, and my happiness has never been more complete. God sent me you, and I can truly feel your love as strong and right for me as mine is for you. We are the best example I can think of for the term "meant to be"!

I have always loved and always will love you, my beautiful, wonderful, and amazing Lisa.

The Wall

There are six steps to building a stone wall. This is not the only kind of wall there is to build, but let me speak to this for a moment.

The skill level involved is "hard." Stone is heavy, difficult to move, and it often pinches fingers. The cost is "much," roughly $800 every ten feet. The time it takes is "as long as it takes." (How high will the wall be?)

First, you must prepare the footing. This involves digging a trench where the wall will be set: the foundation. Next is laying the base course. This is done by setting the first stone then placing the next one next to it and so on until the first course is laid. Repeat this on the opposite side, and top it with mortar in order to solidify the base course. After this, you must build up the wall. At this stage, you simply lay stone after stone on top of one another, continually filling in with mortar, creating a sturdy wall that will last a lifetime or longer.

The last three steps are to "mark" the stones to cut, "cut" the stones (giving the wall its shape), and "tool" the joints, which is the finishing act.

My dearest Lisa, your life has taught you how to build a wall. Although you have experienced joy at times, peace on occasion, and love not nearly enough, you have lifted the heavy stones that have pinched your fingers and bruised your soul. You have paid the high price of anguish and depression for the materials in your wall. It has been over forty years in the making.

The footing was prepared, which involved digging a trench, the scarring of such an innocent, pure, and loving heart. At such an early age, life began teaching you how to build a wall.

The base course was laid, and the wall began to be built. Stone after stone, one after another, what was once the most beautiful, caring, giving, and loving spirit was being walled up and sealed away.

Lisa, as I ponder God's plan for me concerning you, one thing is perfectly clear. I am to dismantle the wall.

There are actually two ways to bring a wall down. One way is to hammer it apart—destroy it. The other is to gently, with care and consideration, clear away the mortar and remove each stone one by one.

I am here to help you take each stone down one by one. My love for you is the tool required to clear away the mortar holding your wall together. My hope for us and genuine desire to nurture healing in your heart will be the tools needed to remove each one of life's stones from the wall that encompasses you. My longing for an uninterrupted, full, and joy-filled life with you, my true love, will be the cleaning agent that brings restoration for our joined hearts.

God alone can and will restore our souls, our spirits, and His plan for us.

I love you with all that I am.

Therapy

When you tell me that you become anxious outside your comfort zone then tell me that you are comfortable with me, it is a sweeter sound to my ear than a favorite song of my youth. To know that I am that place where you feel most at ease makes me feel like I have found my purpose in this life.

I always want to be that person who can stand next to you, know that you are beginning to feel nervous, and gently take your hand in mine, ever so lightly caressing to reassure you that you are not alone. When you can't catch your breath, I will gently kiss your cheek with the calming kiss that signifies, "I am here to help you breathe." When you feel the pressure of others' stares on you, I will put my reassuring arm around you, letting you know that you will never again have to bear the burden of insecurity, for those stares are on us.

Together, we will develop, heal, and weather any storm that comes our way. Together, we are the best therapy for each other that money could not possibly buy. I love you in the way that the word *love* conveys the most complete, compassionate, caring, rewarding, rich, and receiving emotion and covenant I can offer in the English language.

God Created Us

"So God created mankind in His own image, in the image of God He created them; male and female He created them. God blessed them… God saw everything that He had made, and it was very good."

God, with great wisdom and creative knowledge; in the perfection of His plan, created man and woman for each other, and He placed a blessing on that creation. He saw his creation, and it was very good!

God created us, you and me (Brad and Lisa), and He placed His blessing on us. God looked on us, and I believe He said, "They are meant to be very good together." When God designed and formed me, He must have already had your design in mind because we were designed to fulfill God's plan for our lives together.

My love for you has been within me since my youth. Before I even realized what it meant, my love for you was being cultivated.

Like Adam and Eve, we took matters into our own hands and were made to leave the garden. Unlike Adam and Eve, we have been allowed the high honor of tasting the joy of the garden once again.

Lisa, my wish is to work with you in this life, to learn your heart and mind, and to be a comfort, security, and satisfaction for you. You are the desire God has put in my heart. You are the flame that burns so bright before my eyes. You are the soothing breeze that calms my soul.

Your beauty was created for me to behold as the enticement of your affection. Your gentle spirit was created as a safe haven for me in times of despair. Your steadfast devotion has been placed in you as a lighthouse to ever guide me to you when I've lost my way.

God created us for each other, and it is very good. I love you!

A Quickie

It's exactly what you think. A love thought jumps into my mind, and suddenly, I am flushed, discombobulated, excited, and wanting to hold and kiss you, stroke your hair, and whisper sweet nothings in your ear. It can happen anytime or anywhere, and I am helpless to do anything about it. My love for you, I now declare!

A Prayer

Dear Heavenly Father, Lisa and I humbly come before Your throne with adoration and praise in the name of Your Son, Jesus Christ. We offer up the sacrifice of praise as we take joy in all the work of Your hand upon us.

Please lead and direct our path, for it is one path that is the product of two paths joined together by You. Our lives are now one life lived out together for Your glory. May we always remain humble in our attitude, grateful in our hearts, and joyful in our spirit as we follow Your leading and walk in the knowledge of Your Word.

Your Word tells us that You are our shepherd, that we should not want. You, Heavenly Father, are our protection and deliverer. We put our faith and hope in You.

Help me, Lord Jesus, to cherish the gift You have given me in Lisa, to love her as no other can, and to be the gentle, caring, and nurturing spiritual leader that You require me to be. Please help me to be what Lisa needs.

I also pray that You continue to bring healing (physically, emotionally, and spiritually) to Lisa in the way only You can. Help her, Lord, to receive the love and affection You have placed in my heart for her. Continue to work out Your plan for our life.

In Jesus's name, amen.

Sleeping on Me

When we embrace, it is one of the most comfortable feelings I've ever known. It is security, support, and sweet sensuality. However, when we are simply lying next to each other watching a movie, and I begin to hear that soft rhythmic breathing and I feel the warmth of your breath against my chest, I know that you have drifted off into that so-peaceful sleep that only lovers share. "When two are one and comfortable" doesn't begin to describe the feelings they feel for each other. This is the embrace that I remember from so long ago and that I have longed for so long. When I gently caress your forehead and ever so lightly run my fingers through your hair, you let out the softest little whimpers that let me know you are dreaming of me. When I hold you as you sleep, I know that I want to hold you forever.

You Make Me Feel Terrible

When I wake up without you, I feel terrible. When I eat breakfast without you, I feel terrible. When I go to work, I am separated from you, which feels terrible. When I spend hours with you in loving embrace then have to leave you, I feel terrible.

You have a way of occupying all my thoughts all the time. You keep me in a state of constantly running to you or at least wanting to run to you. No matter what else I do, you occupy some part of me that never turns off.

When I am enjoying time with my daughter, I am still silently counting the minutes, hours, or days until I will see you again. Does this make me terrible?

No! It makes me a man who knows he is in love. I am terribly in love with you!

A Prayer

Dear Heavenly Father, I come before You this morning in humble adoration. This day, I give You thanks once again for giving back to me the love of my life. I have been broken, and You have mended me. I have been lost without my true partner in life, and You have brought back the light of Lisa's love to find me. Your Holy Spirit illuminates my path. My heart has been downtrodden, and You have restored joy to my heart through unity with the one You created for me. Thank You, Lord, for all my trials and blessings.

Heavenly Father, be with Lisa and me as we enter into this Easter season. Help us to remember that Your love is the greatest love. Help us to be a light in the darkness and a blessing to those around us. In Jesus's holy name, amen.

Orgasm

"Intense or paroxysmal excitement: the rapid pleasurable release of neuromuscular tensions at the height of sexual arousal."

Lisa, you bring orgasm to my life. When I think of the feelings you bring out in me, the thoughts you provoke in me, and the absolute love for life you inspire in me, I can only describe it as a peak pleasurable experience and explosion of emotion. You make my life experience orgasmic!

I know the word *orgasm* typically refers to the rapid sexual release of muscle and emotion, but I believe there is no better way to illustrate the impact your physical, emotional, and spiritual being have on every aspect of my life.

Lisa, the word *love*, as we know it, as beautiful as it is, as pure and encompassing as we believe it to be, does not adequately describe what you are for me.

In my heart, you and I have belonged to each other from the beginning. There has not been me without you.

A Gas Station Rose

Upon first inspection, one might surmise that the gas station rose is just an inexpensive sidetrack around taking the time and investing the effort to find the "reputable" florist who would select the finest and freshest of roses. The florist would then hand-deliver to the front door of one's lover, showing just how much thought, consideration, and love went into this endearing gift.

On further inspection, we see that the gas station rose is the truest gauge of the intent of the gifter to his lover. The gas station rose says, "It is not about the money but the desire to express love even in the tiniest of gestures." It says, "It is not the size of the gift but the fact that he feels compelled to give gifts, as if to show his courting nature." The gas station rose says, "Even at the end of a hard day's work, while filling up the tank of his motorcycle, he can't help but go into the gas station with giddy pleasure to buy something—anything—for the one he loves." He can't pass by any opportunity, no matter how small, to show his feelings for his lover.

Assurance

Here goes. This may not exactly have the "love note" flavor you have become accustomed to from me, but it is important that you have this as a kind of reference material to return to and read as often as you need.

You asked me a question with tears in your eyes. The look on your face was a look that said you already knew what the answer would be. The thesis of this question had haunted you for decades, yet you could never shake the thought that you knew very well what the answer was.

Life had been thrown so far out of focus those many, many years ago that no life going forward could possibly ever be in focus again. Even though you have experienced moments of joy throughout your life, the overriding emotion has been torment. The question, the answer, the unknown?

When our life together separated, a whirlwind of reasons, whys, and wherefores surrounded us, and no clarity was to be found. But it always boiled down to that one question.

Were you unfaithful in our marriage? Had you wanted someone other than me? Was I not enough? These are just three versions of the same question: the QUESTION.

In your mind, you knew the answer must be yes. It was the only thing that could separate us in your mind. You have spent your whole life trying to reconcile that question and that answer.

My answer? NO! I always will love you! I am so, so very sorry that you have lived with this for so long. I love you always and forever.

I am certain that the action I took in 1989 can only fully be understood by me. It is worth noting that my life was thrown far, far out of focus also at that point. I was never unfaithful to you, Lisa. I cherished you and our marriage above all earthly things, even if I failed in it.

I have always loved you, Lisa. I will always love you, Lisa. You have always been with me, and I have only been unfaithful to the relationships I have had outside of us since us. I also believe that your heart knew this.

I Love You As

Sometimes we say, "I love you beyond words." Let me attempt to tell you how I love you with words. After all, words are what we have to work with, so let me try to put them to work.

I love you as the snowy mountain pass loves the first rays of sunshine come the thawing spring.

I love you as the thirsty blades of grass in the meadow love the first drops of an April shower.

I love you as the tallest oak loves the nourishing soil that surrounds its roots.

I love you as the eagle loves the wind that supports its wings in flight.

I love you as the sands of the ocean floor love the waves that form its contours.

I love you as the earth itself loves the sun that gives warmth in the cold of space.

I love you as the tides of the sea love the moon that affects them so.

I love you, Lisa, as a man created for a woman with a heart that beats for her alone, the one who holds his heart with gentle caress and passionate kiss. I love you beyond myself with all the words I can find.

From the Meadow through the Forest

Two young lovers hold hands as they walk through a meadow on a cool spring afternoon. The air is crisp as a breeze gently blows across the meadow grass, which looks like gentle rolling waves on an open sea. The sky is an exhilarating blue, spreading across the young lovers as if to suggest, the world is theirs and the possibilities of their life together are limitless. The two young lovers hold hands.

As they walk along, the young woman gazes at the young man beside her. She knows that the truest love has entered her life. She will never give up true love! The young man kisses the young woman. This kiss is one of undying passion and devotion. The young man knows there could not, would not, ever be a kiss from another that would rival the spark, the igniting explosive experience that signified the powerful love of this young couple. The two young lovers hold hands with interlocking fingers.

The light spring breeze starts to increase as soft white clouds begin to populate the once clear blue sky. The clouds provide shade while the lovers cross the meadow, approaching a tree line that is the entrance into the unknown. The couple enters the forest fully believing they will find the open meadow on the other side. They clutch each other's hands.

As the two walk hand in hand through the forest, the sunlight struggles to penetrate the foliage above. The man and woman continue to talk as their grips loosen. The ground is stony with short stubbly grass. The forest wildlife has made strange trails that connect and cross over one another, causing confusion and apprehension when trying to decide a correct path to follow through the forest. The man and woman find themselves walking distant from each other as they try to navigate the darkness of the forest; they have strayed on to separate paths.

As they both stumble, stagger, and succumb to the obstacles of this densely wooded forest, they call to each other. Each one is just in sight but always out of reach!

When all the memories have nearly faded away and true love's kiss seems but a fantasy, when the darkest cloud seems to suffocate the rays of the sun that once shone so brightly upon two young lovers, when all seems lost, the meadow appears. The forest has ended.

The older man has been beaten down but not out. The mature woman has the scars of life upon her soul. She stands in the open meadow and looks to the left. He stands in the open meadow and looks to the right. Their eyes meet; their embrace is rejoined. She never let go of true love, and he kisses her, not with a fantasy kiss but with that passionate devotional kiss that only she could return. They have gone from the meadow through the forest. The two old lovers hold hands.

A Phone Call from Arlington

It was February of 1992. I was turning twenty-five, and life was nothing like I thought it would be at the beginning of my midtwenties.

I had restarted a college career. I worked at a video store in an unfamiliar town. I was surviving on candy bars and ramen noodles. I had reinvented myself as a chronic insomniac, and people were beginning to notice that something was wrong with me. What was wrong with me?

Not quite three years earlier, I had divorced my wife, Lisa—the first, best, and only true love of my life. I had felt so inadequate that I had convinced myself that her life would be ruined if I stayed in it. I did the unthinkable.

From the day our divorce was declared "final," I began a slow descent into the nonsense that would become my life. Everything I was or would have been, had I remained with my wife, was everything I could never be without her.

March of 1992 was now here. Dana Carter is a name I will never forget. It was the name of the video store manager. This woman had the discernment to realize that I was deteriorating. She knew the basic facts of my situation, and she instructed me to address the issue. Why she cared was beyond me, but what she said rang true.

After several days of introspection and pondering the outcome of my life if I did nothing and simply carried on as I had been, I decided to make a phone call. This was a difficult thing to do. In 1992, there were no unlimited calling plans. You had to pay for every phone call. I also had no idea what number to call. All I knew was WHO I had to call: my ex-wife.

What was on my mind? Reconciliation! I first called Lisa's mother and explained my intentions, then I asked for Lisa's phone number. After the deafening silence that followed, Donna told me that Lisa lived in Kansas City, Missouri, and gave me her long-distance number. This was the next obstacle.

How would I—a starving, struggling, part-time-working college student—be able to afford a phone call to Missouri long enough to persuade the one person who literally had every reason in the world to answer my call just so she could hang it up?

I asked my store manager for permission to use her office and office phone for one hour in order to make my best effort to bring the only woman who could save my life back to me. Dana gave her consent, her phone, and her office for one hour. Her last words as she shut the office door were "good luck."

I made the call, and my life was changed forever. I did not win her back that night, but I did make her think. After thirty years, she finished thinking it over and did come back to me!

Subconscious Me

When I see you, something happens inside me. I disappear and only you exist. No matter what my task at hand is, all my thoughts go to you: "When will I see you again? How will I get to you? How will you look when I see you?"

Sometimes I think that I am talking to someone, then I realize I haven't heard a word. I was thinking of you. When I touch you, even then, when I think I am enjoying you right in front of me, the subconscious me is even more intoxicated by your aroma, your warmth, your piercing blue eyes. I love you, and subconsciously, I love you even more!

The Mirage

As I walk across the open tarmac, the broad expanse above releases its warmth upon me. The sun beats down with brilliant rays of almost blinding light, causing beads of perspiration to form on my brow.

My eyes squint in a futile attempt to cut the glare coming off what looks like a vast sea of white concrete. My stride is reduced, fatigue builds up in my limbs, and my mind drifts.

Now I see before me what I know is not there. She stands before me, radiant and glorious to behold. Her hair gently blows from a breeze that is not there. Soft brunette tones are accented with the shimmering silver strands that adorn her head. Her eyes, deep pools of blue, cool me as I stand amazed at her beauty. Her shape is voluptuous, curvaceous, tempestuous, and my blood warms to this vision before me. This is not the warmth of the sun but the warmth of desire.

As I walk slowly toward her, her arms reach out for me. I long for her embrace, her healing, soothing touch. I need the balm of her love to cover and protect my heart.

This woman who is not there, this mirage standing before me— so enticing, so inviting—is there after all. She is always there, the projection of my heart on my mind's eye. Lisa, you are that woman. I so deeply love you.

A Short Note

I am thinking of you, my beautiful Lisa! You make my heart jump and my soul sing. Being away from you is the hardest part of my day, but I take consolation in the fact that I am contributing to the future I have together with you.

Patience

pa-tience
Noun:
1. The capacity to accept or tolerate delay, trouble, or suffering without getting angry or upset.

This word does not suffice.

"If I speak in the tongues of men and of angels, but do not have love, I have become a noisy gong or a clanging cymbal" (1 Corinthians 13:1 NIV).

So I am not a patient man. I am a man in love, and patience is only one element in the equation of love that I may exhibit showing my love to be true.

"Love is patient, love is kind. It does not envy, it does not boast, it is not proud. It does not dishonor others, it is not self-seeking, it is not easily angered, it keeps no record of wrongs. Love does not delight in evil but rejoices with the truth. It always protects, always trusts, always hopes, always perseveres. Love never fails" (1 Corinthians 13:4–8 NIV).

Within me, there is a great love for you. I try to live God's Word in all aspects of my life, and I often fail miserably. I think, hope, and believe that my love for you has not failed.

You are the object of my affection! I love you, baby.

726 Steps

Well, 726 is the number of steps it typically takes me to walk across the airport tarmac where I work. I take this walk several times during the day in the execution of my job duties. Sometimes I make this short trek just for the exercise. I make the 726-step journey when I report to work and when I make my homeward-bound exit.

Every time I take those 726 steps, I get lost in thought. I contemplate my faith, I consider my position in life, and I confess to my mind's eye my love for the girl who is love to me. As I walk the tarmac in between those moments of employed labor, my mind swirls, and my heart is more active than all the muscles in my body.

In the time it takes to make this 726-step crossing, I ponder spending the rest of my life with her. I feel, from the joy of knowing, that she will be by my side forevermore, my beautiful Lisa. I meditate on words of love that are so pertinent to our singular situation, and then I let a smile cross my lips as I picture her before me.

Above the smooth concrete of the tarmac float the majestic white clouds that God hung in the sky, seemingly for the purpose of shading my march while they count: "724, 725, 726."

The pavement beneath my feet also counts each of my steps, as if it knows each step is an admiring thought of my true love. Each step brings another cherished memory or an anticipating desire to finish the day's toil and return home to my love.

In 726 steps, I count the hours left in the workday. In 726 steps, I resolve all our issues. I solve all our problems, soothe all our pains, and I proclaim my undying love for Lisa. For you.

I Honestly Love You

> Maybe I hang around here a little more than I should
> We both know I got somewhere else to go
> But I got something to tell you that I never thought I would
> But I believe you really ought to know
> I love you
> I honestly love you
> You don't have to answer, I see it in your eyes
> Maybe, it's better left unsaid
> This is pure and simple, and you must realize
> That it's coming from my heart, and not my head
> I love you

I honestly love you
I'm not trying to make you feel uncomfortable
I'm not trying to make you anything at all
But this feeling doesn't come along every day
And I shouldn't blow my chance
When I've got the chance to say
I love you
I love you
I honestly love you
If we both were born in another place in time
This moment might be ending with a kiss
There you are with yours and here I am with mine
So, I guess we'll just be leaving it at this
I love you
I honestly love you
I honestly love you

(Source: Musixmatch, Songwriters: Jeff Barry / Peter W. Allen, "I Love You, I Honestly Love You" lyrics Woolnough Music, Jeff Barry Int., Irving Music Inc., Woolnough Music Inc.)

These are the lyrics to the popular song by Olivia Newton-John. I use this reference not as a comparison of our story but as a picture of true love and the power it holds.

In the very first verse of the song, we are given the sense that this is a love that will not be fulfilled. However, the love that our artist sings of is so true, dedicated, and honest that she has to declare it! She has to let the object of her love know.

Throughout the song and even to the end, we hear images of impossibility, of futility, of all the weight that sadness can weigh on a person when a dream cannot come true. But I am not speaking of dreams here. I am speaking of love in my own way, declaring my love for you, Lisa. The singer lets us know that these three simple and pure words, when uttered in honesty, override—no, overrule—all the logic and reasoning of the head. These three words overcome all the awkward and uncomfortable feelings that life has instilled in us. These three words: "I love you." I honestly love you.

I believe that these three simple, sure, and sincere words are the most powerful words in any language ever uttered by man, mankind, and even the Creator God toward His creation. "I love you" is a phrase not to be given or taken lightly.

When Olivia Newton-John sings this song, she conveys the idea that you need not respond, you need not react. There is no condition attached. I just have, right now, the opportunity to say "I love you" with a pure and honest love. And if I let this moment pass, I will regret it for the rest of my life.

She makes it clear that the only reason she is able to proclaim her love in the face of calamity is because this isn't that casual love we hear so often in everyday life. She says, "I love you. I honestly love you."

Lisa, I love you. I love you. I honestly love you!

I Think I Know

I think I know what I need to do. I have told you that I cannot say that I didn't love you. I have told you that I cannot say that I wanted our marriage to end. I have told you that I wanted what was best for you. The thing is, only I can understand or make sense of those statements.

I have said that I understood what you went through, but that's simply not the case. I accepted and agreed with what I thought you must have been going through (but that is not the same thing). I have told you that I did all I could, but that is not true. I could have and should have waited. I should have endured. I should have stayed, until death would we part. I was supposed to pray with you and read God's Word with you. I was supposed to protect you from all harm, including the harm done to your heart.

I have told you that I never cheated on you, but the fact that I listened to anyone other than God, you, and my own heart in the matter of divorce did certainly cheat us out of our marriage, our home, and the children we would have raised there. I ended our family before it ever had a chance to live.

We read in Mark, "But at the beginning of creation God made them male and female. For this reason, a man will leave his father and mother and be united to his wife, and the two will become one flesh. So, they are no longer two, but one. Therefore, what God has joined together, let man not separate… Anyone who divorces his wife and marries another woman commits adultery against her. And if she divorces her husband and marries another man, she commits adultery" (Mark 10:6–9, 11–12).

Lisa, I confess to you that I alone did separate what God joined. I was the culprit in this unrighteous act. I confess to you that every relationship I had with any woman after our marriage, to whatever degree that relationship might have been, was an adulterous act against you and a sin against my Heavenly Father and the Holy Spirit. The marriage I entered into after our divorce, even though it was years later, should not have happened, and I am only now fully able to see that. I have been wrong about everything. I have only allowed myself to see things through the tinted lens of my own reality.

I did want out of our marriage in 1989 because I was too shortsighted to see that things could, and surely would, get better. I allowed my own desire for happiness to override the true joy our marriage would have produced over a lifetime of going through and overcoming trials and tribulations that are a part of every righteous act, marriage being one of the greatest.

Lisa, I confess my guilt under a veil of shame. The mistake was mine, and you were blameless. I failed to cherish that wonderful gift that God gave me, and I plunged you into a lifetime of misery. Now all I can do is ask you to forgive me. I do love you, and I will be yours if you will still have me.

What the Future Holds

What does the future hold?

I hold your face in my hands and feel your tenderness course through my veins as I gaze into your sparkling sapphire eyes.

I hold your head against my chest, and my heart begins to compose a love song with no outro.

What does the future hold?

I hold your hand and am reminded of two young lovers united against all odds. It is the act of security, safety, and surety.

I hold you in my embrace as if to signify that I will never let you go. Emotions can't keep us apart. Opinions can't keep us apart. My embrace is my undying pledge that I will hold your love for eternity.

What does the future hold?

The future holds the mystery that is the rest of our life together. The future holds the culmination of our past and present, that wonderful new beginning! The future holds promise. It holds us!

I Miss You

I miss you as the girl I wooed when we were so young.

I miss you as my first and only wife.

I miss the life we could have had together.

I miss the family we should have had together.

I miss all the laughter that would have filled our home—the laughter of you, me, and the children we would have known.

I miss all the time we would have spent playing with our kids.

I miss the unity we would have shared in raising our children.

I miss the hard times we had. They were a blueprint for how I would do everything so very differently than I did before.

I miss the opportunities I have had when failed to act.

I miss how we used to sing in church.

I miss our ministry as youth pastor and wife.

I miss our entire life.

I miss you and me without regrets.

All these things I miss are true, but one thing I will never miss is saying "I love you."

A Letter to Mike

Dear Mr. Mitchell

I am writing this letter in an attempt to bring some kind of relief to my mind and ease the pain my heart has adopted in your absence. While I rejoice in your heavenly reception, it has left a void in my life here in this mortal realm. There are some things that I feel a need to commit to paper. Perhaps after I have had this posthumous conversation, my thoughts will clear, and the burden won't feel so heavy.

Mike, you were one of my oldest and dearest friends. I have loved you as a brother in the Lord and even as my own brother. We have helped each other through the twists and turns of life. At times, the struggles we faced, together or individually, seemed insurmountable. They were not. There were also so many times that laughter ruled the day. We have both been accused of being willing to do anything for a laugh; I believe this to be true.

I recall all the many conversations we have had about friendship, morals and values, manners, language, comedy, theology, the ministry, God's calling, the Holy Spirit, martial arts, addiction, women, music, drugs and alcohol, philosophy, miracles, healing, and finally this: When making the perfect batch of brownies, was margarine as good as butter? We have had a lifetime of questions and answers, and I feel richer for it. Sometimes when I speak, I even sound like you, or did you always sound a bit like me?

I have seen all the stages of your life, and I am proud to call you brother and friend. I have always been able to count on you, except for the time you promised to tutor me in trigonometry. You would have known all the things I have been writing about. But there is something that you never knew, and that is what I need to tell you about at this time.

Back in 1988, you attended my first wedding. I was married to Lisa Diane Collings—my first, best love. You saw one of your best friends become a husband. It was such a joyous time. Lisa, myself, and our whole youth group thought Lisa and I would be together forever, but this is not what happened. Not a year later, Lisa and I were divorced. Mike, you helped me through one of the toughest times in my life.

In 2002, you were the best man at my second wedding. I know that you must have known that I still held Lisa somewhere in my heart because through the years, you were the thread that held Lisa and me together. Our lives, Lisa's and mine, were so far apart; we had lost track of each other. But you had a way of staying in touch with the youth group of our past, which made you the one I would always ask, "Do you know how Lisa is doing?" You never gave me too much because you knew that I still held on to Lisa, and being my best man, you felt your duty was to my current marriage. You would always ask how my current wife and daughter were doing. You were a great friend.

Mike, you passed away believing that Tricia and I were a happily married couple. What you never knew was that, just weeks before your passing, Tricia told me she wanted a divorce, which she followed up with "I want you to move out." I did move out, and shortly thereafter, you left this mortal coil.

What follows is the miracle that God performed in Lisa's life and mine. I would venture to say that aside from you being freed from cancer and receiving your glorified body, this was one of the best things your death initiated in my life. With your rapidly deteriorating state and the demise of my second marriage, a sense of urgency possessed me. I decided to no longer try to guess what Lisa's life had become. I reached out to her through Facebook. Ironically, I friended her—asked her to be my friend. Lisa replied surprisingly quickly with "Hey, Brad! How are you? It's been a minute! LOL." And just like that, we were reunited! Lisa knew of your condition and expressed her concern for my state of mind and heart. We began to talk.

Just less than a month later, I informed Lisa that you had gone on to heaven. Lisa conveyed her wish to go to the funeral service, and although my heart was aching for you, it leapt at the thought of actually being able to see her in person after so many years of separation. The day of your service came, and as I tried to console guests at Church on the Hill (a task I was failing miserably at), a woman walked through the front door. The sun behind the woman created a halo effect around her as she entered the bustling room. Immediately, I knew it was Lisa, and I made my way to welcome this angel from my past with a hug. The hug was magical for me. For a moment, I actually forgot that I was at a funeral. Then I forced myself to let go and say hello. We talked briefly in the foyer, then she went in to be seated.

I didn't tell Lisa that I was going through divorce. I didn't tell anyone. I was there to honor you and help comfort your family in their time of grief. I thought that if I could just cultivate a friendship with Lisa, my happiness would be satisfied. I also knew that I still loved her and that I had never stopped loving her. At the graveside service later, I was able to talk more with Lisa, and she communicated that she wanted a renewed friendship with me. Our talk wasn't long, but it was meaningful, and it was a new beginning.

For the next several months, we chatted on Messenger, texted, and talked on the phone. I finally told Lisa that my wife was divorcing me, and then the miracle continued. Lisa told me that she had been in a broken marriage for the past thirty years and that she was leaving. We were both going through divorce. I at once thought of reconciliation! We talked increasingly. We prayed together. We were defiantly becoming friends again. Then one day, Lisa asked me about a time in our past, a time just before she had remarried, and I had called her in an attempt to reconcile. That attempt had not succeeded, but now she was asking if I remembered that phone call and if I meant it. I told her that I did remember the call and that I certainly meant it. That was when I knew that she still loved me.

We decided to meet in person. We met, declared our love for each other, and began the therapy that was in every conversation we had over the rest of the year.

What you need to know is this: my love for Lisa never died, nor did hers for me. Tricia and I are no longer married, and Sam chose to live with me. Lisa and I are engaged and intend to be remarried. Without authoring a whole other paper on all the aspects of marriage, let me sum it up this way. I feel like everything is finally being put right, and I can't help noticing the timing of all that has happened over the last year.

Mike, my dear friend and brother, your death has been an instrument of the rebirth of my life with Lisa. It is a life that should have been all along and now will be. Rest in peace, brother, and we will all rejoice again at the marriage supper of the Lamb!